Power
Etiquette

Power

Etiquette

What You Don't Know Can Kill Your Career

Dana May Casperson

AMACOM
American Management Association
International

New York · Atlanta · Boston · Chicago · Kansas City · San Francisco · Washington, D.C.
Brussels · Mexico City · Tokyo · Toronto

*This publication is designed to provide accurate and authoritative
information in regard to the subject matter covered. It is sold with
the understanding that the publisher is not engaged in rendering
legal, accounting, or other professional service. If legal advice or
other expert assistance is required, the services of a competent
professional person should be sought.*

Library of Congress Cataloging-in-Publication Data

Casperson, Dana May.
    Power etiquette : what you don't know can kill your career / Dana
May Casperson.
       p. cm.
    Includes index.
    ISBN-10: 0-8144-7998-7
    ISBN-13: 978-0-8144-7998-8
    1. Business etiquette. 2. Business communication. I. Title.
HF5389.C37   1999
395.5'2—dc21   98-49831
                                                          CIP

Printing number

20 19 18 17 16 15 14 13

Dedication

To my mother, Ruth Sohler Dibble, who instructed me in all my good manners and continues to encourage and teach me.

Contents

Acknowledgments

I wish to express my sincere appreciation to Laurie Harper, my agent, for her interest in the subject, her wise and thoughtful guidance, and her encouragement, which kept me on task! I thank her for taking my hand and showing me the way to fulfill my dream of publishing a book. One cannot imagine the support she gave me personally and to the project. To Ellen Kadin at AMACOM who was enthusiastic about the book from the beginning. I thank her for all her help.

To Vera Allen Smith and Joyce Allen Logan for their editorial wizardry and who gave this book the form and flow I envisioned. They taught me how to build a book. No one could ask for more talent and dedication than they gave me. To Natalie Omholt, my illustrator, who eagerly took pen in hand to quickly interpret and create what was needed. To Robert Haley who took time from his busy schedule to read and edit the original manuscript. To FormPrint Design, Robert Scott, Ann Lindsay, and the technicians for their fine work and willingness to produce photostats in rapid time. And to my husband, Steve Casperson, who stood close by with encouragement and love, sitting alone while I sat with the computer!

Power Etiquette

S uccessful business relationships rely more than ever on personal contact. Courtesy, politeness, and service are necessary in all our business and personal relationships. *Power etiquette* is the ability to learn and use social skills to transact business with thoughtful consideration. This book offers suggestions on ways to treat your clients and business associates with courtesy and respect. It will help you become a more considerate, competent, and credible person.

You will learn appropriate and polite ways to relate to others in the business world. Whenever you meet with clients, you present an image of your company and the way your company conducts its business relationships. Your poise and professionalism affect all your business and social relationships. You want to be your best, bring out the best in your clients, and cultivate lasting business relationships. Your skills in relating to people have never been more critical to your success. Your ability to relate positively and professionally to your colleagues and associates will place you in the forefront.

Our business environment is dominated by technology: videoconferencing, computers, answering machines, facsimile (fax) machines, complex voice message systems, fax-on-demand, e-mail, pagers, cell phones, and more. Although these tools are designed to speed our transactions and improve efficiency, they do not replace the need for personal contact nor free us from the responsibilities of good communication. To the contrary, we have more communication tools to operate, more responses to make, and less time to do it in!

We are under pressure to do more in less time, without sacrificing the quality of our interactions with colleagues and clients. Our business survival depends upon our knowledge and practice of good manners. Business etiquette is not about being rigid or stuck within the confines of rules. Etiquette is better defined as guidelines for conducting business with ease, style, and confidence. So why is there so much resistance? It could be the word itself—*etiquette*—a French word that conveys an air of sophistication and, perhaps, stuffiness. It is difficult for some people to spell or even pronounce, so why bother with the "rules" of etiquette at all? Because when you properly acknowledge others with whom you conduct business, deliver what you promise, keep in touch, build the relationship, and offer competent service and a reliable product, people will look forward to working with you and will recommend you to others. People gravitate to those who are kind, considerate, thoughtful, courteous, respectful, and interesting.

You, your employees, and your colleagues present your company image wherever you go, during business hours and afterward. You are an extension of your company and the way it conducts business. Whether you are at the grocery store, health club, or on the golf course, you and your company's image are visible. Be aware of how you conduct yourself; your manners are always showing. Your behavior affects your career in both obvious and subtle ways. Your behavior and manners, good or bad, can open or close the doors to your success. You never get a second chance to make a positive first impression.

Good manners are always in style. They change somewhat with demographics and time but they never disappear. Whether you are sitting for your first interview, re-entering the workplace, taking a new position, or wanting to polish your professional presence for career advancement, your knowledge of business etiquette is essential.

This book offers you the skills you need to use every day. Your "manners tool kit" weighs nothing, is invisible until used, and provides you with the confidence, competence, and comfort to meet new situations with poise and grace.

Some of the situations described may already be part of your own experience; others will be new. Learning how to handle situations appropriately, with proper business etiquette, will begin to prepare you for your next encounter. These are real experiences by real people. Fill your "manners tool kit" with new and necessary skills. The etiquette skills you develop will be useful to you throughout your career and in your personal relationships. Soon your business etiquette will become *Power Etiquette*. Power comes from knowledge. Knowledge builds confidence and confidence builds leaders. Be a leader by being confident and knowing what to do; practice *Power Etiquette*.

Business Etiquette: Test Your Knowledge

❖ *At a business meal when do I discuss "the business"?*

"The business" may be discussed after the entrée plates have been removed. How to conduct business during meals is discussed in Chapter 3, Meal Manners.

❖ *When a valet hails the taxi, who enters first, my client or me?*

The host enters the taxi first; the valet closes the door after the guests enter. Further discussion of transportation can be found in Chapter 9, Business Travel.

❖ *Is it appropriate to pay transportation or parking expenses for the attendees at my business meeting?*

The attendees had the options not to attend or to submit their travel/parking expenses to the company. You are not responsible to pay their expenses. Additional information on this question may be found in Chapter 7, Preparing for the Job.

❖ *When a client gets a parking fine while at my office, should I pay it?*

Unless your client followed your advice to park in an illegal parking zone, you are not obligated to pay any fine. Provide parking suggestions for your clients, particularly if parking is difficult. Additional information on this question may be found in Chapter 7, Preparing for the Job.

❖ *After the meeting is it appropriate to "talk business" in the restroom?*

There are times when informal settings, including restrooms, provide the atmosphere for thinking and talk, therefore the restroom may be an appropriate place to discuss business. The responsibilities of the host and the guest are discussed in Chapter 3, Meal Manners.

❖ *Am I expected to stand and shake hands when people enter my office?*

An expression of courtesy and respect such as rising and shaking hands is always appreciated, although not necessarily required. Meeting and greeting people is discussed in Chapter 1, The First Impression.

❖ *After work, a friend and I are going directly to dinner. Can I wear a special necktie or fancy blouse to work?*

Fancy or evening dress is best saved for after work hours. Wear your daytime business attire for work; carry the evening attire and change into it after work. Information on your business wardrobe and appropriate clothing for business functions is discussed in Chapter 2, Your Business Wardrobe.

❖ *A holiday gift was sent to my office. Is it appropriate to e-mail a thank you note?*

It is better to write a personal thank you note even if you must telephone for the postal address. E-mails lack the personal touch required of a thank you for a gift. Gift giving is discussed in Chapter 10, After Hours. Sending a note of thanks is covered in Chapter 4, Write It Right.

❖ *When should I send a handwritten note?*

A personal, handwritten note is appropriate for all thank you correspondence. Writing notes and letters is discussed in Chapter 4, Write It Right.

❖ *When I meet a business colleague after work hours are there topics we should avoid discussing?*

Leave important business topics at the office. Avoid office gossip, complaining about coworkers, and discussing confidential business or business finances. The subject of appropriate conversation is discussed in Chapter 6, When You Speak.

❖ *What should I wear to a "black tie optional" event my employer asks me to attend?*

Ask your boss how formal she wants you to be as a company representative. Normally, a man is required to wear a dark suit, white shirt and tie, or a tuxedo to a black tie event; a woman may wear a short cocktail dress or evening pantsuit. Information on what to wear to formal events is presented in Chapter 2, Your Business Wardrobe.

❖ *Whose name do I say first when introducing my employer to our new client?*

Make the introduction using the client's name first, followed by your employer's name. How to make proper introductions is detailed in Chapter 1, The First Impression.

❖ *I am a woman executive who meets foreign clients in our corporate offices. Should I shake hands when greeting them?*

Generally, you should rise and shake hands whenever you meet clients. Because there may be exceptions, you may need to do some culture research before extending your hand. Greeting new people is discussed in Chapter 1, The First Impression. Cultural courtesies are mentioned in Chapter 8, Office Finesse.

❖ *I annually attend a conference that benefits the entire office. Should I bring gifts to the staff from my travels?*

A token gift is always appreciated. Select something from the conference like items with the conference logo or items from the city. In addition, remember to send a postcard to the office staff. Appropriate gifts for business colleagues and staff are discussed in Chapter 10, After Hours.

❖ *What is an appropriate holiday business gift for clients?*

Consider your position in your company, the client's position in their company, the client's industry, and your corporate gift budget. Edible or consumed products such as food items, candles, or plants are always appropriate. Appropriate gifts for business clients are discussed in Chapter 10, After Hours.

❖ *Whom do I gift? When and for what occasions?*

Make yourself familiar with your corporate policy and gift budget before you give gifts. Gift those who have helped you succeed during the year. Appropriate business gifts for different occasions are discussed in Chapter 10, After Hours.

❖ *What is a self-introduction and when do I use it?*

A brief statement about who you are and what you do is your self-introduction. Whenever you introduce yourself, you have an opportunity to share this information and build a new relationship. Introductions are discussed in Chapter 1, The First Impression.

❖ *My name is frequently mispronounced when I am introduced. How do I correct my introducer?*

Repeat your name when acknowledging those you are introduced to. Later, you may want to speak privately to the introducer, as he may not know the correct pronunciation. The importance of names is discussed in Chapter 1, The First Impression.

❖ *After an interview how long should I wait before I call and ask if I am hired?*

During the course of the interview ask about the hiring process and when the final hiring decision will be made. Call on the specified day. Interview follow-up is covered in Chapter 7, Preparing for the Job.

❖ *How should I greet people when I am running the booth at a trade show?*

Shake hands and make eye contact; a personal acknowledgment goes a long way. How to meet and greet people is detailed in Chapter 1, The First Impression.

❖ *At a company party I drank too much and flirted with the boss. Should I apologize in person or write a note of apology?*

Avoid drawing attention to your errant behavior. If you openly embarrassed your employer, send an apology for having caused embarrassment. Business entertaining and office parties are discussed in Chapter 10, After Hours.

Chapter 1

The First Impression

*B*usiness etiquette is the art of knowing how to behave in a given situation and knowing how to interact with people. Etiquette is the guideline for knowing how to behave appropriately in all situations. Good manners make good business. It is not enough to know your company and product well. You must also know how best to meet people and make introductions, how to dress for the occasion, how to use your business cards properly, and how and what to gift, among other things. Your knowledge encompasses your leadership style, your communication, and your behavior in different business settings. Good manners are not optional; they are essential tools you must use every day. Improve your skills if you wish to advance, rather than sabotage, your career. In this and the following chapters, we will examine many aspects of etiquette and how they apply, particularly in business situations. All these skills are important to your success and will be essential components of your *Manners Tool Kit.*

In today's business world I often hear, "Manners are not important these days" or "I am who I am. I have been successful in business, so why should I change?" There is a deceptively simple answer: etiquette is power. Good manners open doors that position and money cannot. We all have room for improvement. Using the skills in your *Manners Tool Kit* will help you to be polished and professional; others will perceive you as knowledgeable and confident. Your colleagues may seem willing to overlook your blunders now, but be assured, they won't overlook them indefinitely. At critical points in your career, you may be passed over in favor of someone who practices Power Etiquette.

Learning the "rules" of business etiquette is easy; they are 80 percent common sense and 20 percent kindness. But what does that mean? If you are looking to your coworkers for guidance, you may be disappointed.

With insecurity in the job market and competition everywhere, you can't afford to rely on your instincts or "to do what seems natural." Formal education seldom includes much, if any, training in business etiquette. We learn our manners from our family, friends and, later, our colleagues. Manners are skills that must be continually practiced and updated.

ATTITUDE

Relating to others is what etiquette is all about. The many ways in which you relate to others begins with your attitude. Your style of connecting with others, your way of communicating your respect of others, and your behavior toward others are all reflections of your attitude. Your attitude and your professional image help form the first impression others have of you.

Attitude is a personality trait you continue to develop throughout your life. Your attitude pervades your actions and is evident in every detail of your life and how you relate to others. Your attitude is evident in your body language, how you complete tasks, your attention to details, your consideration of those around you, how you take care of yourself, and in your general approach to life. Attitude begins on the inside and shows on the outside. You can improve your attitude by creating pleasant surroundings, playing calming music, meditating, or sometimes even by wearing bright colors. Colors, sounds, and smells contribute to one's sense of well-being. You must be happy at what you do, be content within yourself, create a pleasant environment within which to live, and continue to learn new things.

Attitude and self-discipline work together to make the good things happen for you. Good attitude is a cornerstone of *Power Etiquette*.

THE FIRST GREETING

Should I rise and shake hands when someone comes into my office?
Yes. When someone from outside your company enters your office it is a gesture of respect and courtesy to rise, move from behind the desk, and shake hands.

Your handshake speaks loudly about your professionalism, credibility, and confidence. It shouldn't come as a surprise that your abilities may be judged by the five-second handshake. The handshake is an important contact or physical link between two people. A firm handshake conveys confidence, assurance, interest, and respect. A limp handshake can send the opposite message.

Your handshake communicates a powerful nonverbal message before you speak. A firm handshake conveys "I am interested in you and confident in my business skills," whereas a weak handshake may be interpreted as "I'm unsure of myself and I'm uncomfortable being here and meeting you." Eye contact and a smile during the handshake are also essential because they show attentiveness. The initial connection between two individuals is an opportunity to establish rapport and positive chemistry. An immediate bond develops from the touch of a hand and sets the tone for conversation and future business association, leading to a productive relationship.

All cultures have customary gestures of a handshake, kiss, hug, or bow that signifies a greeting and the commencement of an encounter. The unspoken greeting is an act of respect and an acknowledgment of another person. The handshake is the first physical connection we have with the person and serves as the bond. It is always appropriate to shake hands in the business setting. Gender is not a determinate on whether to shake hands or not. By shaking hands easily, often, and graciously, you actually influence your peers to shake hands more often.

Use your right hand to shake hands and don't squeeze too hard. Keep in mind that a handshake should be firm, not bone crunching. Be especially considerate of seniors (and others) who may suffer from arthritis; return similar pressure to theirs. Your hands should touch with web to web (between thumb and forefinger); wrap your fingers around the other person's hand (see Figure 1.1). Shake hands vertically with the thumbs up, facing one another squarely.

Your handshake should be brief, yet long enough for both persons to speak their name and a few words of greeting. Look directly at the other person and smile. Think about your handshake and the message you convey. Practice with a colleague who will be honest with you and then shake hands often!

Figure 1.1
Illustration of the proper handshake.

As you develop and practice your handshake, there are some bad habits you will want to avoid. Clasping just the fingertips, pumping the hand up and down excessively, or rotating the hands with one hand on top of the other can be uncomfortable and may leave a negative impression on the other individual. Likewise, flapping the elbow or locking the elbow straight should be avoided. Be aware of your body language as well. It is best to face the person squarely and look at them when you shake hands. Standing angled away from the other person or looking away may leave the impression that you are not interested in them or their business.

A handshake is almost always appropriate. Shake hands whenever you are introduced to someone, whenever you introduce yourself to someone, and whenever you say good-bye. You will also want to shake hands when someone enters your office, when you encounter someone from outside your office, when you are introduced to others from outside the company, and when you leave a meeting attended by people from outside your company.

Do I rise and shake hands when a woman enters the office or boardroom?
Yes, as a gesture of respect and goodwill, rise and shake hands with anyone entering your office, whether male or female.

There is no gender distinction when using your handshake except in specific situations where your client's religious or ethnic background may be a consideration. Be observant and follow the clues of those around you. The conservative approach is usually safest. If you are a woman meeting foreign guests, check your culture guide to learn the specifics about women's role in business. When you need an answer quickly, call the nearest appropriate consulate or embassy.

GETTING ACQUAINTED

Introductions serve many purposes in business. An introduction may acquaint individuals with one another. An introduction may serve as an opener for conversation when approaching a new acquaintance or it may begin a telephone call to a prospective client. We use two kinds of introductions every day: (1) the introduction of two or more people to one another, and (2) the introduction of one's self, the self-introduction.

Learn to introduce individuals properly so that it will be easy and comfortable. If you appear to avoid making introductions, you leave a negative impression with all involved. You will appear unprepared and unprofessional, both traits that can quickly undermine the image you want to project of yourself and your company. Plan and practice your introduction just as you would an important presentation.

Introducing People to One Another

There is an art to introductions. It is important to make the introduction even though you may be confused about which individual you should introduce first. If you forget someone's name, apologize politely and say that you have forgotten his or her name. They will most assuredly repeat their name for you. Be gracious and make an introduction even if you feel slightly awkward. The individuals involved will be grateful that you made the effort.

To make an introduction properly takes practice, keen observation, and some sense of age and seniority. It is important to understand who is being introduced to whom. The purpose of an introduction is to give people an opportunity to get to know one another. During the introduction, you can help to facilitate easy and comfortable conversation between the individuals by weaving appropriate information into the introduction of each individual.

> *"John Brown, I would like you to meet Linda Jones, our recently elected chairperson. Ms. Jones, this is Mr. Brown, senior manager at Widget Express. Ms. Jones recently completed a four-day hike in Yosemite. Mr. Brown coached a championship youth soccer team last season."*

The introducer knows that Ms. Jones was a university soccer player and that Mr. Brown enjoys hiking. By including a comment about Ms. Jones's recent outdoor experience, you are providing helpful conversation openers. The same is true for the comment about Mr. Brown's soccer coaching. The individuals thus introduced have the responsibility to follow through with questions or comments. Offering some subjects of mutual interest in the introduction will help the two people to converse. Most people are comfortable talking about subjects with which they are familiar and are eager to share with people of similar interests. You can also help start the conversation by asking questions about the individual's interests.

In the business world, defer to office seniority and age. Gender is not a factor. An introduction is normally made in a logical order. Knowing office seniority and company titles will simplify the introduction. The older or more senior person is mentioned first.

- ❖ Introduce the younger to the **older.**
- ❖ Introduce your company peer to **a peer in another company.**
- ❖ Introduce a junior to **a senior executive.**
- ❖ Introduce a fellow executive to **a client or customer.**
- ❖ Introduce a nonofficial to **an official person.**

As indicated in the above list, mention the name of the boldfaced person first when you make an introduction. First mention the name of the **higher-ranking person, senior executive,** other **company executive, client,** or **official** followed by the name of the other individual. Explanations of who the people are facilitates further conversation. For instance, you would state your company's vice president's name first when introducing her to the sales manager of another company. Remember that gender and social status are not factors in business. If you are introducing two people of the same title or of unknown seniority, introduce your acquaintance first. Always state the more senior person's name first, even if he is the younger person.

To introduce a junior to a senior executive:

"Ms. Senior Executive, I would like to introduce Ms. Junior Executive."

To introduce an individual to a senior executive:

"Mr. Don White, president of our company, I would like to introduce Mr. Sam Short, sales director for XYZ Company."

Titles are used in introductions when an older person, a person with a professional title, or a person with official rank is being introduced. Official titles are used for public and government officials even after they have left office and for retired military personnel as a courtesy and expression of respect. A former member of the U.S. Senate or House of Representatives, presidents, governors, judges, and mayors also continue to use their titles. You should also always include the title of clergy in your introductions.

To introduce an individual to a senior executive:

"Cindy Day, I would like to introduce John Thorn. Mr. Thorn, Ms. Day is our newly promoted vice president of marketing. Ms. Day, you will find Mr. Thorn full of exciting tales of his travels around Asia."

To introduce a person with a title to another person with a title:

"Senator Diane Wise, I would like to introduce Representative Lynn Green, a friend from California District 57. Representative Green, Senator Wise has recently retired after serving several terms in the U.S. Senate."

To make a casual introduction between close colleagues and family:

"Jack Adams, I would like to introduce my daughter, Jennifer Jones. Jennifer, this is Jack. Jack grew up in Montana. Jennifer started her college career at the University of Montana. I am so proud of her accomplishments. This year, she hiked the entire Appalachian Trail."

This introduction includes information that will be of interest to both persons and will serve to start a conversation between the two.

To introduce your boss or the president of the company to a client:

"John Client, I would like you to meet our president, Susan Boss. Mr. Client is our new client from Fresno."

Introductions are not complicated when you follow these simple guidelines. An introduction is a courtesy to help two people feel more comfortable when they meet for the first time. Even if you think two people may have met previously it is a good idea to introduce them to one another. You demonstrate your professional acumen by extending the thoughtful gesture of making an introduction. When you know one person, but have never seen or only briefly met the other, it is acceptable to ask the unknown person's name and then make the introduction.

Don't let your uncertainty about whose name to say first lead you to avoid making an introduction altogether. It is more proper and polite to make the introduction anyway. Normally, failure to name the higher-ranking person first is less of a fault than failing to make an introduction at all.

If you are chatting with a group and a newcomer approaches your group of acquaintances and you are the only one who knows the person, it is courteous to include the newcomer by introducing him or her to the others. A newcomer may be uncomfortable standing by and wondering how to become part of the conversation of your group. You may interrupt during a pause in the conversation to make the introduction. Another courteous way to include a newcomer is to turn your body slightly toward them so they become part of the circle of individuals chatting. The body language indicates that they are welcome to the group.

To introduce an individual to a group:

"Bill, it's good to see you. I would like to introduce my colleagues from North Bay World Trade: John Wood, Peggy Rogers, and Jeff Smith. This is Bill Jones, owner of Widget Wheels."

By including information about the person being introduced, the introducer enables any one of the three others to pick up the conversation. Usually someone knows someone in the same business and will make a remark, which quickly engages the newcomer in conversation, and will ask questions that ease the newcomer into the conversation and helps him feel comfortable.

Keep the following pointers in mind whenever you are making introductions:

- ❖ Avoid using nicknames unless that name is the person's business name.
- ❖ Use full names (first and last).
- ❖ Use titles such as Dr. for a Ph.D. when you know the person always uses one.
- ❖ Always use a dignitary's title, even if they are retired.
- ❖ Speak slowly and clearly so each name can be heard.
- ❖ Make a brief statement about each person's interests or recent accomplishments.

The Most Important Word

Our name is one of our most valued assets. Everyone likes to be remembered and to have her name pronounced and spelled correctly. Many business deals have been lost because the contact person could not remember the buyer's name from one meeting to the next. How do you feel when someone addresses you by the wrong name? Making the effort to remember people's names and to pronounce them correctly has many rewards. Your clients will perceive you as someone who cares not just about business, but also about the people involved. Personal relationships strengthen business relationships.

Despite our best efforts however, we all occasionally have problems with other people's names. We all forget names at one time or another;

it's a common problem and not something to fret about. When you are making an introduction or are in conversation but cannot remember a name, simply ask. A statement like, "I am sorry, I have forgotten your name" or "your name has momentarily slipped from my mind" is sufficient.

If you are a visual or kinesthetic learner, it may help you to remember the name and how to pronounce it if you write the name; if you are an auditory learner speak the name at least three times. If you are still unsure about the pronunciation, ask the individual to repeat it again for you.

Try this experiment: ask a person to repeat their name. They will speak it normally. Ask a second time and they will speak it louder. Ask a third time, and they will speak louder and s-l-o-w-e-r. This pattern happens over and over. People really want to help you pronounce their name correctly. Whenever you are unsure of the name, pronunciation, or spelling, ask. This test is also evidence of another phenomenon you will want to be aware of. Many people you meet will be of ethnic or cultural backgrounds different than your own, and their names may reflect these differences. Sometimes people get confused when others don't understand them and begin to speak louder. If the problem is the result of language pronunciation or comprehension rather than hearing loss, getting louder will only serve to aggravate the problem. It is better to speak slower at a normal volume.

Most everyone wants to have his or her name pronounced correctly and will help you with pronunciation when you ask. In today's business world, you are likely to conduct business with individuals from diverse ethnic and cultural backgrounds. Many of their names will be unusual in your experience. Ask them to help you pronounce their name correctly. Your name may also be unusual to many others. Use the same patience with others that you would hope for.

If your name is frequently mispronounced, develop a pleasant way to correct it during the introduction. Gracefully correct the error, without calling undue attention to it. You want to give others the opportunity to learn the correct pronunciation.

There also will be times when you may meet or greet someone who does not readily use your name. It's possible they have may have forgotten your name or are uncertain of its pronunciation. Tell them your name to remind them. To avoid embarrassing yourself by using the wrong name or when you're not certain of the name, make an introduction by asking for names. If you are in a situation in which you are not introduced, take the initiative to introduce yourself. Your name will be pronounced correctly, and you'll ease any awkwardness others may feel at not knowing your name. There is no need to call attention to the oversight by asking to be introduced, just take the initiative and introduce yourself.

A married couple I know has a creative procedure they use when they meet someone they haven't seen in a while or whose name has slipped their collective memory. When Debbie realizes her husband can't remember the new person's name, she steps in and shakes hands. "Hi, I'm Debbie. I don't think you and I've met. What is your name?" In this way, she coaxes the person's name from them so both she and her husband now know the person's name.

Remembering a name may challenge the best of us. Try these simple techniques:

- ❖ Listen carefully to the names of individuals as they are introduced.
- ❖ State the name as soon as possible. "It's a pleasure to meet you, Mr. Smith." If you can use the name three times early in the conversation, you have a good chance of remembering it.
- ❖ Ask for the name to be repeated.
- ❖ Connect the name with something common to you. Maybe the name is the same as that of a school friend or a favorite fictional character.
- ❖ Notice some unique feature of the person and connect it with the name.

Some people also have difficulty remembering how others prefer to be addressed. Many names have more than one part: Mary Ann, Jo Lyn, and even my name, Dana May. A gentle correction can usually solve the problem, "Actually, I have a dual first name as in Mary Ann. I am known as Dana May." Avoid correcting the individual who is making the introduction directly. Keep in mind that other people's names are as important to them as yours is to you. What impressions do you draw of others when they mispronounce or forget your name? They may be drawing the same conclusions about you. Perhaps they perceive you as failing to pay attention to details or being sloppy in your business. For the most positive results, make a diligent effort to correctly introduce and address people you meet.

Some people are especially sensitive about being properly addressed; others are more tolerant. In our casual world, we often overlook the fact that people have last names and titles. We can never assume that a person wishes to be addressed by their first name; to do so implies familiarity, which is not always appreciated. You may not know the person well, you may be inadvertently abbreviating their name, or you may be calling them by the wrong name altogether. To be on the conservative side address a person with a title of Mrs., Ms., or Mr. until you are advised otherwise. Errors in using people's names can sour business dealings very quickly, particularly when you are working with individuals from ethnic or cultural backgrounds with which you are not very familiar.

Introducing Yourself

We often find ourselves in situations in which we need to introduce ourselves to others. This is an opportunity to meet others and an opportunity to share information about yourself. Your self-introduction always includes your full name and what you do. You may even wish to include a hint to help others remember your name more readily.

> *"Hello, my name is Dana May Casperson, a southern name with a ghostly twist. As a speaker, writer, and tea aficionado I assist people in polishing their professional skills."*

Your self-introduction may vary according to the setting in which you use it and the people you are meeting. A self-introduction need only be a fifteen- to thirty-second description of who you are and what you do. A brief, finely tuned introduction is especially useful when networking or when you are beginning a conversation with a new acquaintance. Be selective about the words you use to describe your work. Work to refine your self-introduction so it will both provide information you wish to share and also interest others. Plan what you want to tell people about yourself. You may wish to type your self-introduction on a card and carry it with you. Practice your self-introduction often. It should sound natural and spontaneous. Try your introduction out with friends or colleagues and ask their opinions. No doubt you will get some very helpful and practical comments. Continually fine-tune the wording and emphasis. If what you say doesn't sound the way you want it to or is not generating conversation, change it until you are confident that it will generate the response you want.

> *"Good afternoon, I am Nancy Kelly from Sacramento Nails. I pamper you with manicures and pedicures to relieve the stress in your life even if only for an hour or two."*

> *"Good morning, my name is Andy Lewis. My company, CMD Products, offers convenient, lightweight trade show displays to make your booth setup easier."*

In those situations when someone asks you what you do, you can use just the last part of the self-introduction, describing what you do. You may change the introduction to make it more relevant to the person or setting.

Your self-introduction is a window of information that may serve to draw others into conversation. You have provided a subject (or two) others may want to know more about. They may want to learn more about what you do. Use your self-introduction whenever you introduce yourself or whenever you want people to know something about you or the kind of work you do or services you offer. Many business self-introductions give you an opportunity to briefly promote yourself, what you do, and your company.

If you are seated next to someone at a meeting or meal, a positive way to begin a conversation is by introducing yourself. This is the time to use your preplanned self-introduction! Normally, the other individual will then introduce him or herself and say their name and the conversation will begin. Who knows, the person you've just introduced yourself to may be your next client!

Helping people feel comfortable in different situations is an important part of good etiquette. In properly making an introduction or self-introduction you have an opportunity to help people meet one another, to help someone relearn a name they've forgotten, or to talk with someone you would like to know or who wants to know you.

Body Language

Body language is a form of nonverbal communication by which our gestures, expressions, and body position and movement convey unspoken messages. Sometimes the message expressed by body language contradicts the verbal message. If you say you are prepared and confident and then you shuffle into a room with your chin on your chest, you convey a different message. Before you say a word, you have sent a message that you are reluctant and unsure of yourself. You have undermined your own credibility by allowing your body language to contradict your words. Your tone of voice can also convey nonverbal messages. For instance, when you claim you are not angry by yelling, you create a mixed message that will confuse your listener.

How others perceive you is critical to your success or failure. Be aware of the messages your body language is sending. Perhaps you think others don't notice, but such small things as a yawn, a glance at the clock, or fidgeting with a pen says more than you can imagine.

Make an effort to make your body language reflect calmness and control. Work on controlling your positive body language. If you feel nervous, practice self-talk about being calm and be aware of controlling your gestures and posture. When you jiggle your foot, tap your fingers, and crack your knuckles you display your nervousness or discomfort about the situation you are in. Instead, breathe deeply, sit or stand straight without slouching, and make eye contact with others. They will think you are calm and collected and before long you will be! When you're speaking you can help yourself to keep your listener's attention by drawing your listener's eyes to your face with an engaging smile and pleasant facial expressions.

Positive Body Language

❖ Make eye contact.

❖ Hold your head level.

❖ Keep your chin up.

❖ Sit straight in your chair, without slouching.

❖ Stand straight with both feet on the floor.

❖ Allow 18 inches of comfort space around you when conversing with others.

❖ Walk with grace and ease.

❖ Smile often.

PERSONAL GROOMING

Good grooming is an important part of how you present yourself. To look your best consistently practice good grooming habits everyday. You must bathe daily. Clean hair and clothing help us to look and feel our best and thus to perform to the best of our ability. Body odor is offensive and is a very personal issue. If you believe a coworker has body odor and is unaware of the problem, the matter should be brought to the attention of the personnel manager or discussed with the individual privately. You must tactfully, honestly, and straightforwardly explain the problem and offer suggestions for correction (daily bathing, daily clothing changes, sending the clothing to the cleaners, deodorant use). Individuals often are not aware of problems like body odor or overly strong perfumes and aftershaves. The conversation may be personal and even awkward, generally, however, people are appreciative that someone took the time to inform them.

Maintaining clean, healthy, and attractive hair is also an important part of your daily grooming requirement. Corporate policies vary regarding hair. Men may want to be aware of any policies on facial hair as well. Hairstyles and lengths vary widely, depending upon where you work and the industry in which you work. More conservative industries like banking and finance may require women to wear their hair shoulder length or shorter and men to wear their hair off their necks. Industries that are less conservative may have more liberal policies. The same is true for facial hair, which includes beards, mustaches, and sideburns. Policies on facial hair vary by geography, industry, and company. In any case, your hair and facial hair should be clean, neat, and trimmed regularly. Many individuals enjoy coloring or styling their hair in creative ways. Purple streaked hair or very unusual hairstyles might not be good choices in some work settings.

Be aware that body piercings and tattoos may limit your opportunities and impact how others perceive you. While negative perceptions may be unfair, they are a reality of the business workplace. You may need to cover tattoos and de-emphasize piercings to better present yourself in a professional or more business like manner.

Be certain to comply with company policies. Opportunities and promotions may be withheld or lost if you fail to follow the accepted guidelines.

Your hands and nails should also be clean and manicured. Avoid rough and broken skin around the nails, chipped nail polish, too long nails, and broken and/or jagged nails. Avoid letting your hands become too rough or dirty looking. Your hands and how you keep them say a lot to your clients and potential clients. Protect your hands by wearing rubber, latex, or other work gloves when necessary. Your new client may have second thoughts if the first time he shakes hands with you, your hands still look like you just changed the oil in your car.

Give yourself a quick check in a mirror before you leave the house to make certain that zippers and buttons are secured, clothing is lint-free, no undergarments are showing, and there are no fabric splits.

No matter how much effort you put into building good grooming habits there will still be times when you lose a button, damage your hose, or break a nail. To combat these little emergencies, I suggest you keep some personal supplies on hand both at home and in your desk or locker.

Comb and brush	Extra socks or hosiery
Nail file and nail clippers	Lint brush
Hand cream	Facial tissue
Toothbrush and paste	Premoistened towelettes
Makeup/shaving kit	Breath mints
Nail polish/lacquer	Safety pins
Hair spray	Small sewing kit

Chapter 2

Your Business Wardrobe

*B*efore you speak a word, your clothes have already spoken volumes. The first impression is made in only a few seconds and may follow you indefinitely. You present your professional polish, competence, and knowledge in a few brief seconds, then fill in the gaps with words. The professional presence you bring to the business world has tremendous, although unspoken, impact on the business transaction.

Be attentive of your total being. Your presence is being observed when you enter the office, go for an interview, enter the boardroom, participate in a videoconference, make a presentation, are working a room, or are socializing with colleagues. Assumptions about your business ability are made on the spot, sometimes based solely upon your appearance and manners, and your product or services may be negatively affected if the client forms unfavorable impressions of you before you even have an opportunity to speak.

Your wardrobe, personal grooming, and body language all serve to create your "personal professional package." That is, all aspects of who you are—what you wear, how you move, how you look—all work together for your benefit or to your detriment. Each aspect affects how a client or potential client perceives your ability to conduct business professionally.

Today's society is transient and fast paced. We are programmed for quick sound bytes and visual bytes. Your personal message is delivered in five seconds. Clothing sends one such message. It is a message of status, personality, character, refinement, discernment, and success. You are the message of your business and how you dress, walk, speak, write, and interact with people may be all a person sees of your business or company, service or product. You have a responsibility to send the best professional message you can to be successful.

Plan your business wardrobe now. Begin by always having two *great* outfits or suits ready to wear. Keep all the components—suit, shirt/blouse, socks/stockings, shoes, and accessories—cleaned and ready to go at a moment's notice. I call these the no-brainer outfits. They are smart, sharp, fashionable, conservative, and are tailored to fit you well. Of course, you should be wearing them rather than "saving" them for the right occasion, but be mindful that when you hang them in the closet they must again be ready to go on a moment's notice.

Hints for "No-Brainer" Dressing

- ❖ Purchase complete outfits that work together.
- ❖ Purchase all the components for an outfit at the same time, including accessories and hosiery.
- ❖ Coordinate pieces that can be mixed together for different looks.
- ❖ Select the outfit and hang it outside the closet the evening before.
- ❖ Take time periodically to examine and repair your garments.
- ❖ Make regular trips to the cleaners.

Although you may not think of yourself as one, you are always a salesperson. You are selling your expertise and business acumen. The way you dress shows respect for yourself, your profession, your associates, your company, and the products or services you offer. Your appearance is your "visual résumé."

In business, as in our personal lives, we are required to dress differently for various occasions. Think of the world as a stage where your part in the play can make or break the play's success. You plan your costume and rehearse your actions to make your whole presence successful. So think of yourself as an actor—plan your wardrobe, practice your body language, choose your words with care, and the lasting impression you leave will be positive.

The Business Wardrobe

After work, my friend and I are going directly to dinner. Can I wear a special necktie or fancy blouse to work?
Your after-hours activities should not dictate your work clothes. Change after work for your dinner date. Take a blouse or shirt and tie suitable for evening to work with you.

Demographics and your particular field of business define the appropriateness of what you wear to work everyday as well as what you wear for business events. It is always safe to dress conservatively. Geography, climate, and season help determine fabric colors and weights. Dress with a touch of individual flair whenever possible; wear current fashion and color. Being trendy is not important, but being current with accessories, especially shoes, color, and fashion accents indicates that you are aware of what is fashionable. Your necktie width, design, and the type of knot indicate that you are current. The way you wear your tie makes a fashion statement and that statement may be perceived as the way you look at business. Are you up-to-date with what is happening in the world and in your industry? Being current implies that you are up-to-date in your business knowledge as well.

Careful consideration should be given to wardrobe planning. When selecting and purchasing clothing, think about where and when you might wear it, how often, and whether you have other garments that coordinate with it. Check that the colors match or coordinate with other garments (socks, shoes, jacket, and trouser/skirt). You want to be perceived as competent and professional by your client and colleagues—will the garment contribute to that perception or undermine it? Women need to be especially wary of garments that may reveal too much body, especially low necklines, bare midriff tops, shorter skirt lengths, and sleeveless blouses. Choose blouses with long or to the elbow sleeves and select skirts of knee length or just below. Men need to avoid showing too much body as well; wearing too many shirt buttons open may reveal more than is appropriate in a business setting.

Men's clothing selections are also important. A man's necktie should reach just to the waistline. If your tie ends in the middle of your chest, it's too short. Big and tall men may purchase ties made especially for them in longer than average lengths. Large patterned print shirts may not look well on slim or smaller men. Check your appearance in the mirror. Men's socks should match the color of their slacks or shoes for business dress. White or bright socks break the linear look of the leg and are distracting. Purchase socks that extend above the pant cuff when you are seated.

Choose accessories with care; jewelry, scarves, and neckties need to be selected to complement the individual and the wardrobe. Accessories that are too bold or swing too much, such as bright neckties or long pendant-style necklaces, can be distracting to others. Noisy bracelets with charms or dangles that hit work surfaces can be dangerous as well as annoying to coworkers. Offices use a wide variety of equipment in the course of business; beware of catching jewelry, scarves, long hair, or neckties in office equipment.

To build a business wardrobe try this formula: $4 + 4 + 4 = 40$. This formula is not a purely mathematical one, but represents how these pieces work together to create more than forty complete outfits. Forty outfits equate to a different outfit every working day for two months. Women have more options by using both slacks and skirts. Four tops, four bottoms, and four shirts or blouses will combine to give you forty days or more (eight 5-day weeks or 2 months) of workday attire. It works! By keeping your wardrobe simple, you have fewer decisions to make when you're selecting what to wear for the day and you always know that you will look appropriate (see Figure 2.1).

Dressing well takes careful planning and thoughtful color choices. It is becoming easier, however, to buy coordinated pieces that conform to the $4 + 4 + 4 = 40$ formula because manufacturers are producing, and stores are displaying, mix and match coordinated clothing pieces for both men and women. The formula works by combining three compatible solid colors and one print that goes well with the solids. Select a top and bottom as a suit. For women a three-piece suit (skirt, slacks, and jacket) will work for one "unit." Add another suit of another color and a top and bottom of a print or texture that work with the other solid colors. Men need to select one or two suits, a jacket or two, and two slacks of different colors and fabrics (see Figure 2.2). All the colors must

Figure 2.1
Wardrobe illustration for women.

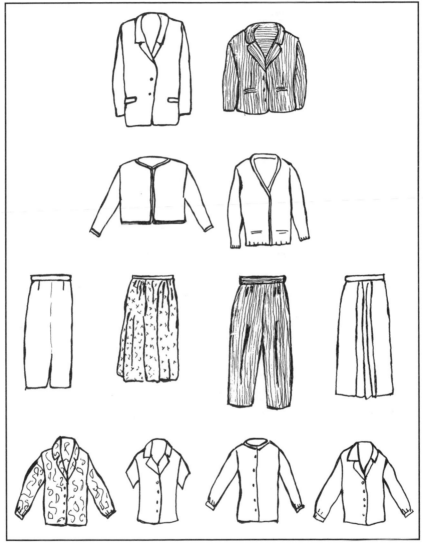

work well together. Shirts should be of various colors and patterns to co-ordinate with all the tops and bottoms. Neckties should also coordinate with several combinations. Select new ties periodically if you wear a tie everyday. Select conservative and fun ties to fit the various occasions of your business life.

Figure 2.2
Wardrobe illustration for men.

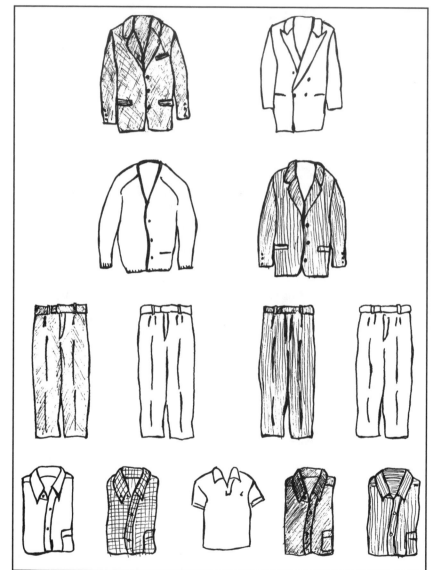

Choose neutral colors (navy, black, brown, beige, burgundy, or gray) for the basic pieces, which are the tops and bottoms. Add more color for the shirt or blouse pieces; use your individuality for the shirts, and pizzazz for the accessories. Your unique style and expression of your interests sets you apart from others. You may like a particular color and wear accessories of that color. Perhaps you are a weekend cyclist or golfer and choose bicycle or golf themes for lapel pins, neckties, or print fabrics. Some men wear only bow ties as their signature. Some women wear hats. Maybe you like flowers; wear one on your lapel every day! Tops can be various styles of jackets (for women, a cardigan sweater). You will be pleased when you practice this art of dressing. Your closet will seem neater and less crammed, and your mind will be less distracted by thoughts of what to wear.

Even in a working environment that accepts casual as the regular dress code, there may be subtle differences in dress from one department to another. When Matthew was interviewing at a high-tech corporation, he noticed that the research and development department personnel wore jeans and tee shirts; while the people from the production department wore collared shirts tucked into their jeans and belts. Be aware of the dress where you work and adjust your wardrobe appropriately.

If you are starting a new job or have moved to a new area of the country, observe how others dress for work, especially those working in your industry or type of work. You may also get some ideas by reading the local paper. If you are unsure of what kind of clothing is appropriate, ask your supervisor.

CASUAL DAY

What to wear for Casual Day is becoming more of a dilemma than was originally expected. *Casual Day* is a term signifying that casual dress will be allowed on a specified day. Some companies have a Casual Day every Friday, some have their Casual Day on the last Friday of the month, some have a floating Casual Day that is announced monthly. The idea behind Casual Day was to remove some of the pressure of always having to look businesslike and formal at work. The intention was to raise morale and increase productivity by easing the dress standards on select days. The idea of eliminating the "business look" for everyday has become popular with some companies while other companies have rejected the Casual Day idea altogether.

Casual lifestyles demanded casual work wear. The day began as a trial on Fridays, when many were starting to think about the weekend and no work. Some corporations made Wednesday their Casual Day. Some companies made it every day. Many workers felt that because they were not seeing customers, were behind a desk or telephone, or were at the computer doing their business, there was no need to dress up for work. The concept was great, but in practice it needed guidelines. Businesses today are continuing to grapple with the task of defining dress code guidelines. Of course, the clothing industry liked the concept because it created a new line of clothing—Casual Day business clothes. Casual business clothes include cotton slacks and skirts, sweaters, casual shoes, and relaxed design lines. Some workers find it just as difficult to decide what to wear to work on Casual Day as on other days. Some forgot the day was casual and went to work dressed in their regular business attire.

Management found that their employee's interpretation of casual varied dramatically. Clothing ranged from beachwear and spectator sportswear to casual dress up. Prior to Casual Day, workers knew the corporate dress code and dressed accordingly. Casual has created a new set of rules.

Corporations have even hired consultants to help workers determine and define the meaning of business casual. Newspaper ads and magazine articles have attempted to clarify the business casual dress code. Some clothing manufacturers have even marketed their specific line of clothing as the definition of "casual" business wear.

Business Casual Do's and Don'ts

- Do wear hose or socks.
- Do wear collared shirts.
- Do wear belts in pant loops.
- Don't wear denim or shorts.
- Don't wear sleeveless blouses or shirts.
- Don't wear barefeet sandals; open-toed shoes may be worn with hose.
- Don't wear sheer fabrics.

❖ Don't wear open, unbuttoned shirts or low necklines.

❖ Don't wear midriff-baring clothing.

❖ Don't wear exercise clothing.

Those who dress casually are often less productive than their colleagues who are dressed more professionally. Those who dress for business work better and are well received by colleagues and clients. Many individuals are now choosing traditional business attire, a tie and jacket, instead of such casual dress as denim, shorts, or sandals, for work.

Think "business professional" when you dress. Client expectations for professional services are ever increasing. Your client's perception of your expertise comes in part from your appearance.

Dress appropriately for your profession to increase your credibility. A heavy equipment salesman may not need to wear a suit and tie to visit his contractor client. He will need to wear slacks with a belt and a collared shirt, tucked in. He may choose clean work boots over dress shoes for sales calls in the field.

Casual Day is becoming less popular. Perhaps it's time for your company to reconsider its policies regarding casual dress. As Casual Day becomes attached to holidays and community events any occasion becomes an excuse to dress casually. The critical consideration is whether casual dress reflects the image you want your clients to see. What do you think of your bank when you see your bank manager at the office in jeans and a tee shirt?

Businesses need to seriously look at their corporate image and consider how their clients perceive their professionalism in terms of appearance. Business relationships are based on trust, confidence, and personal attention. The client's good opinion and impression of you is vital to your company's success and to your own. Are you meeting their expectations?

If your business is considering implementing a Casual Day or wanting to amend the dress code, develop written guidelines and distribute it to employees.

Casual Day Guidelines
❖ Clothing should be appropriate for the business service or product.

❖ Consideration for the employee's movement and actions during the workday (lifting, moving boxes, bending, sitting).

❖ Clothing that is clean, pressed, and free of stains, tears, and patches.

❖ No workout clothes, beach wear, or sports clothing.

❖ If clients will be in the office, consider more standard business dress.

Newscasters seem to have a unique approach to dressing for work. Since most people see them only from the waist up, they pay special attention to how they look from the waist up! If you see most of your clients from a desk, as a receptionist might, look sharp from the waist up. I am not suggesting that you go as far as the television celebrities who wear jeans and sandals from the waist down, but do look carefully at yourself from the waist up.

SPECIAL BUSINESS OCCASIONS

The invitation to an event generally indicates the appropriate dress for the occasion. Whether the event is a cocktail party or a barbecue, held at home, in a restaurant, or at a country club, guests are expected to wear appropriate attire. Often the indication for suggested attire is printed at the lower right of the invitation. If you are unsure of the type of event, when you respond to the invitation you may ask if the event is informal or formal. The host will happily answer your questions. After all, he wants you, as the guest, to attend and be comfortable. If he is vague and answers too casually for your liking, ask some specifics about the location, size of the event, and suggestions for attire.

Check your invitation to be certain whether you alone were invited or if your spouse or significant other was included. The host should be sensitive and informed about each guest and their living arrangement, especially if the invitation is for an intimate gathering. If your name is the only one on the invitation, you must determine whether you want to attend alone. An intimate dinner party, for eight to twenty guests, may not allow room for your personal companion. If it is a cocktail party or an informal company party, there may be room for more guests. Always assess the type of occasion and ask the host when you respond to the invitation. There are times when the host has overlooked the detail of including "others" on the invitation. The host should never assume the person would enjoy attending alone just because they are not married. If, as the invited guest, you are unclear about whether you must attend on your own, call the host to acknowledge the invitation and gently ask about the possibility of your companion attending.

Couples should coordinate their clothing so that they do not appear as the odd couple. One should not be wearing sparkles while the other is in Casual Friday attire. Your professional image is always important even when the occasion is a nonbusiness function. When a couple's clothing is not coordinated, they give the impression that they have not communicated. This does not mean that colors and style must match from the same style page; it does mean that you both should be in the same chapter. If she is wearing a cocktail dress, he should be wearing a jacket and slacks, not jeans and a tee shirt. Likewise, if he is wearing a suit and tie, she should be wearing something dressy rather than stretchy pants with a sweater.

The Company Party

Company parties are events hosted by the business for clients and customers. Spouses may be included, but usually children are not. Company employees are the hosts and should attend. The host is responsible to see that the guests have food, are introduced to other guests, and are enjoying themselves. This is the time to get to know your clients in a social setting. Generally, business deals are not made, but business subjects may be mentioned. This is the time to learn about your client's interests outside business. Company parties may be held in the office as an open house or as a catered event at a restaurant or hotel. Wear the same clothing you would normally wear for work or dress it up a little.

The Office Party

Office parties are those social events held outside regular office hours in which employees and sometimes their spouses and families participate. These may be catered holiday parties, annual parties, or company picnics. Office parties are frequently held at the office, at a local restaurant, park, or at a company official's home. The party may be in the same city or miles away. These events provide a relaxed environment for mingling among coworkers and family members. Many times, there are attendees you've never seen before. Several offices may be combined for the event.

A company I've worked with holds its annual picnic at the boss's house a hundred miles from some of the branch offices. Although there is no obligation to go, there is an implied need to attend to meet the boss, upper management, and employees from other offices. An office party at the boss's home gives you the opportunity to see how the boss lives and to assess whether his personal values, as evidenced in his lifestyle, match corporate policy and values. Extravagant personal living and bare-bones corporate operations are in contrast. You might wonder if corporate profits benefit only the CEO to the possible detriment of the future of the company and its employees.

Generally, there is no spoken obligation to attend an office party, but it does provide you with an opportunity for friendly, relaxed conversation with coworkers and with important people in your company. If you cannot attend, it is important that you respond to the host with your regrets. You need not explain why you cannot attend.

The clothing you wore to the company's summer barbecue is not appropriate for the five-course meal, of course. Your outdoors casual jeans and shirt need to be replaced with slacks and shirt or dress and skirt for the company party or dinner party. Gentlemen would need a necktie when attending a more formal party. You may ask the host about suggested attire when you accept the invitation.

Women

* ❖ Don't wear something that is too tight. Tight clothing can be perceived as flirtatious and unprofessional.
* ❖ Don't wear low necklines. Keep your professional image professional, even at an office party.
* ❖ Don't wear fur and diamonds if you think you are in line for a raise. Fur is politically incorrect in some geographic areas of the United States; if you want to wear fur, you may want to check this detail out before hand.
* ❖ Do dress up your business attire with a beaded sweater or festive vest.

❖ Do swap your business pumps for evening shoes.

❖ Do freshen up and reapply makeup. Add a bit more sparkle than you normally wear during the workday.

❖ Do change everyday accessories to ones with pizzazz; make them larger, bolder, and more colorful.

❖ Do add a sparkly hair ornament.

❖ Do consider shiny fabric for the blouse.

Men

❖ Do wear the appropriate shirt for the occasion. White shirts are more formal than colored shirts. Pale colored shirts are more formal than bold or bright colors. Solid colors are more formal than patterned.

❖ Do wear an interesting and colorful necktie.

❖ Do add a complementary pocket-handkerchief.

❖ Do add interesting cuff links.

❖ Do add a festive vest.

Office parties are an extension of work, but with a different tone. Always be aware that your credibility and professionalism are visible. Even when the conversation is not about business you are perceived as the business person you are in the office. Have a fun time, but avoid letting your hair down too far.

Many people who may influence your career advancement and future success see and hear you without you even being aware of them. They all form an opinion of you, based upon your behavior and your words. If you talk too loudly, laugh too harshly, tell off-color, politically incorrect, or racial jokes, or say disparaging things about coworkers or management, you run the risk of damaging your career.

Jim: *What do you think about including Bob? He was at the office party last summer.*

Chuck: *Bob? You don't mean the loudmouth that kept complaining about how hard he had to work on the Hillsdale Project? I sure don't want him on my development team.*

The "Bob" in the above conversation will never know why he was not considered for this new development team. He thought he did a fine job on the Hillsdale project and other projects as well. It's too bad he talked a little too loud and complained a little too much about his work at an office party where the vice president of research and development was also a guest. Always consider the impact your words and actions may have on your career, even in what may seem like a relaxed party situation. Practice your best manners and exercise proper etiquette at every opportunity.

What to Avoid at Business-Related Social Events

❖ Drinking more than one alcoholic drink.

To prevent being perceived as "holier than thou" by declining a drink if your guest orders one, ask for mineral water with a twist of lemon or lime. It will come from the bar and it will look like an alcoholic drink without being one. Juice, ice tea, or "virgin" (no alcohol) drinks also work for this purpose and help put your drinking guest at ease. You can also make arrangements with the cocktail server or bartender in advance to serve your drinks "virgin." (Be sure to tip!)

❖ Being loud.

❖ Being flirtatious.

❖ Telling offensive jokes.

❖ Revealing confidential information about the company or employees.

This can be difficult in settings in which the only thing you may have in common with the other person is that you both work for the same company. Be cautious about discussing company or personnel issues.

Casual Wardrobe

Your casual wardrobe will include your weekend wear, after-hours clothing, and Casual Day attire in fabrics of cotton and cotton blends, knits, polyester, linen, and rayon. Casual garments are less structured in design than business clothing, generally unlined, and loose fitting.

Men

❖ Slacks of cotton and cotton blends worn with a belt

❖ Collared shirt, turtleneck, knit polo shirts with collars

❖ Socks, either white athletic or colored

❖ Slip-on shoes, canvas shoes, or athletic shoes

❖ Zippered jacket and/or sweater

Women

❖ Skirt of soft fabric, synthetic, or natural fibers

❖ Relaxed-fit slacks worn with a belt

❖ Blouse with sleeves

❖ Sweater

❖ Socks appropriate for the shoes

❖ Flat shoes

Semiformal Wardrobe

Semiformal events call for attire that is dressier than business but not as formal as a tuxedo. Holiday parties, dinner parties, dinners at hotels and restaurants, catered events, theater, and musicals are all events that may require semiformal clothing. When you are the hostess, you set the tone of the evening. However, if you know that your out-of-town guests do not have semiformal clothing with them, dress down so as not to embarrass them by being more formally dressed than they. Semiformal or informal dress calls for dressy, shiny fabrics with some sparkle.

Men

❖ Dark suit

❖ White shirt

❖ Dark stripe or dark patterned tie

❖ Dark socks and shoes

Women

❖ Pantsuit of shiny, light and flowing, or lacy fabrics

❖ Short dress of evening fabric: sparkly, shiny, light and flowing, or lacy

❖ Mid-calf, ankle-length skirt and top or dress. No floor length hem lines

❖ Dark hose and shoes; flat shoes or pumps of suitable height for women

If the dress has small or no straps, a woman should wear a shoulder wrap, at least during dinner or whenever she is sitting down. From across the dining table, often all that one can see is bare shoulders; this may not be the impression you wish to leave. Be mindful of where most of your evening will be spent, at a dining table, sitting at a concert, or standing at a reception. Use this information to plan what you will wear.

Black Tie

Black tie events include opera, symphony, and theater opening nights. Balls, dinner events, evening fund-raisers, and weddings that begin after 6:00 in the evening may also be black tie occasions. Seasonal variations in dress include color, length of the sleeve, and fabrics. If you attend a dinner party, be cautious of wearing a strapless dress as you may appear to be wearing very little when you are seated at dinner! Black tie dress codes may also vary by geography; check with your host.

Women

❖ Long cocktail dress or evening gown in muted colors, beading, lace, and/or chiffon

❖ Sheer hose

❖ Fabric shoes may have ornamentation or have a metallic, sparkly finish

❖ Small handbag

❖ Evening wrap

Men

❖ Tuxedo (in some regions, a white dinner jacket in summer)

❖ Tuxedo shirt, cummerbund, bow tie, cuff links and studs

❖ Or a dark suit, white shirt, dark tie, cuff links, and studs (acceptable for some situations)

❖ Black shoes and socks

Colorful neckties, cummerbunds and vests are fun, but not always appropriate for business functions. Evaluate the situation. Will there be foreign business guests? Are you the host, the master of ceremonies, or giving a toast? Remember that your business reputation is always on view.

White Tie

White tie is the most formal dress affair. Clothing can be rented for these events for both genders. White tie is worn by the bridal party for formal weddings after 6:00 in the evening, for inaugural balls, debutante balls, and fund-raiser galas.

Men

❖ Tailcoat, called "tails," a formal coat with "tails"

❖ White bow tie

❖ White tuxedo/wing shirt

❖ White cummerbund or vest

❖ Gloves optional, in white or gray, depending on jacket color

❖ Black shoes and socks

Women

❖ Long evening dress (business-appropriate evening dresses are not low-cut, body clinging, or high-slit dresses)

❖ Sheer hose

❖ Fabric shoes

❖ Gloves are optional but appropriate; long white gloves are often worn with a sleeveless dress. (Gloves are considered an accessory to a woman's wardrobe.)

❖ Evening wrap

❖ Small handbag, handheld, no shoulder strap

For white tie events, women wear a floor length dress or flowing chiffon pants. The hem length is longer than for black tie events. This is the event where you can really dress up with glamorous jewelry, fancy hairstyles and ornaments, special shoe ornaments, and furs (if appropriate).

Gloves, Overcoats, and Hats

Some wardrobe items, specifically gloves, overcoats, and hats, need special mention in regards to proper etiquette. These items are more or less fashionable from time to time and region to region. As a result, appropriate wear and etiquette may be a mystery to many.

Glove Etiquette

Women

❖ Gloves are removed when eating. Gloved hands do not hold food or the utensils for eating.

❖ Gloves may remain on for handshaking.

❖ Long gloves should have a buttoned opening at the wrist. Remove only below the wrist, fold the hand portion of the glove and tuck it into the wrist opening. This will leave a small bulge at the back of the wrist.

❖ Glove length, whether short or long, is determined by the length of the sleeve of the gown. If the gown is sleeveless or short sleeved, long gloves are appropriate, if long sleeved, the gloves should be short. Gloves can be wrist, forearm, elbow, or mid-upper arm lengths. Choose the appropriate length in proportion to your dress.

❖ A bracelet may be worn on the outside of long gloves, but never a ring.

❖ Gloves may be worn at any time of the year.

❖ Gloves may be removed after your entrance and placed in a handbag.

Men

❖ Men generally wear gloves for hand protection in cold weather or on white tie occasions.

❖ Gloves are removed when taking off the overcoat and are then tucked away in a coat pocket.

❖ Gloves are removed for eating and drinking.

Overcoat Etiquette

❖ Overcoats are removed when one enters a building or office.

❖ Overcoats may be carried over the left arm.

❖ Overcoats are checked at hotels, theaters, and most restaurants.

❖ The coat checker is tipped if he sits in a booth or cabin.

❖ The choice of overcoat should be appropriate to the clothing. A stadium coat is not appropriate over formal attire.

Hat Etiquette

Men should remove their hats when entering a building. They do not wear hats while they are indoors or while eating. Women wear hats as a wardrobe accessory. Unlike a man's hat, a woman's hat remains on her head at all times. Her outdoor or wet hat is removed indoors. A woman also removes her hat if it obstructs the vision of another person seated behind her.

Chapter 3

Meal Manners

The following quiz on dining etiquette at business functions may serve to open your eyes to some limits in your knowledge of dining etiquette. These questions, and more, are covered in this chapter.

Business Meal Etiquette: Test Your Knowledge

❖ *Should I take a briefcase and/or folders to the dining table?*

Take your business papers, but leave them under your chair or under the table until the entrée plates have been removed. When it is time to "talk business" be careful not to cover the table surface with papers.

❖ *Is it proper to order a glass of wine?*

Many corporations have a no-alcohol policy, and if so, the answer is predetermined. It's generally a good idea to save the wine until after the business is concluded. Although there are some exceptions, alcohol should not be served at a business meal.

❖ *I eat my large meal at midday. Is it proper to order a large entrée at a business lunch?*

Pay attention to your host's suggestions, and select your entrée accordingly. If necessary, you may need to alter your normal eating pattern. If you are the hostess, by all means suggest to your guests that they order a full meal.

❖ *Who orders first?*

The host directs the server to the guests first; the host orders after his guests.

❖ *When do I talk business?*

The primary business talk should wait until after the entrée plates have been removed.

❖ *Where do I put my hands?*

To remember what to do with your hands and elbows, or more specifically, what not to do, follow the easy saying—elbows never, forearm sometimes, wrists always.

❖ *Where is the best place for me to put my cell phone so I can answer it quickly?*

Leave your cell phone in your brief case, turned off. If you must accept an essential call, alert your host or guests when you sit down. When the phone rings, excuse yourself from the table and keep your conversation private and brief.

❖ *What should I do if my fork or napkin falls on the floor?*

Sometimes tables are crowded and utensils do fall on the floor. If this happens, use your foot to move the utensil under the table and ask the server for another. Pick up the napkin unless you will disappear from view of the guests to reach it.

❖ *What should I do if the check is put in front of my guest?*

The hostess should ask for the check, or reach for it first. Make the comment, "You are the guest of company XYZ today."

❖ *What should I do if the check is put in front of me and I am the guest who was invited to this lunch?*

The host should reach for the bill; wait for him to do so. If he does not, suggest to the host that you split the bill.

❖ *Can I remove my suit coat while at the table?*

It is best not to remove your coat unless the host does.

❖ *What should I do if I get food stuck between my teeth?*

Avoid drawing attention to yourself in this potentially embarrassing situation. If you are not able to free the food using your tongue (with your lips closed), then try the napkin.

Well over half of all business is finalized at the dining table. The percentage of business conducted over the dining table is even higher. Among other things, business meals are used for conducting job interviews, getting to know a client, deciding to become a partner in a venture, networking, and signing the contract. All your professional polish is on display at the dining table. All the details, from where you sit, what you order, and how you use the dining utensils to your table conversations demonstrate your respect for others, as well as your courtesy, poise, and style. Never assume that others will not notice or will be understanding of your poor manners. Always be polished in your dress and manners.

TABLE MANNERS

Do some people offend or embarrass you by their eating?
Even your best friends will be reluctant to correct your poor dining habits. Observe how others eat and how they look when viewed from across the table. Think about how others see you.

The concept of fine dining has been downplayed in recent decades. Business people often say to me, "What difference does it make how I eat?" Your business expertise may end here. Your poor eating skills may alienate your client and effectively stall further business with him. There is no excuse for embarrassing yourself or offending the person across the dining table by eating boorishly. Good table manners are simple enough to learn in one meal. We eat three meals a day so we have many opportunities to practice good table manners. Do not ruin your professionalism by handling the fork like a caveman or a child! Basic dining skills are so simple that you cannot afford to ignore them.

It should not surprise you that all your professional polish is evident at the dining table! "All the world was your oyster, but you used the wrong fork." Don't be caught with the wrong fork in your hand or holding it incorrectly.

The Table Setting

The arrangement and number of pieces of silverware are your clue to the menu. If there are three forks (on the left), you know that there will be three fork courses. There could be salad, fish, and entrée *or* salad, entrée, and dessert. (See Figure 3.1.)

The size and shape of the utensil (spoon, fork, or knife) is your next clue. Look at the spoons and knives at the right side of the place setting. Note the size and shape of each; their shape determines their use. Knives should match the forks in size, shape, and number, although the salad knife may not be on the table.

Figure 3.1
The formal table setting.

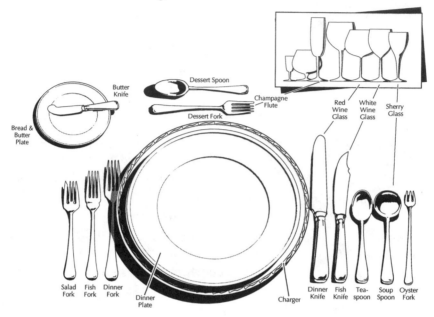

The glasses will be placed on the right side of the place setting. Their size and alignment will be your clue to the number of wine courses. (See Figure 3.2 for an illustration of the various types of glasses.) The number of glasses should match the number of forks and spoons. The bread plate will be placed on the left side of the place setting (liquids on the right, solids on the left). (See Figure 3.3.)

By looking at the table setting, the knives, spoons, forks, and glasses, you can make an educated guess about the menu; at least you know the number of courses.

You may wish to limit your bread consumption. Speaking of bread, take a serving of butter from the butter dish. Put the butter on your bread plate (on the left). Break the bread into two pieces, one bite sized, and spread butter on the small piece. Eat your bread by continuing to break off bite sized pieces, one at a time, to butter and eat.

If the serving dishes are placed on the table, pass the dishes of food to the right. If the food is served by serving persons, the food is generally served from the left and later removed from the right.

Figure 3.2
Illustration of stemmed glasses.

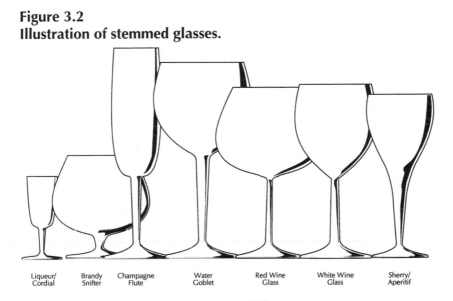

| Liqueur/ Cordial | Brandy Snifter | Champagne Flute | Water Goblet | Red Wine Glass | White Wine Glass | Sherry/ Aperitif |

The resting position, with utensils resting in the shape of an inverted V, indicates that you are not finished eating. The closed position at 4:00 (as on a clock face) indicates you have completed your meal even if there is still food on the plate. (See Figure 3.4 on the next page.) A

Figure 3.3
Illustration of the table setting.

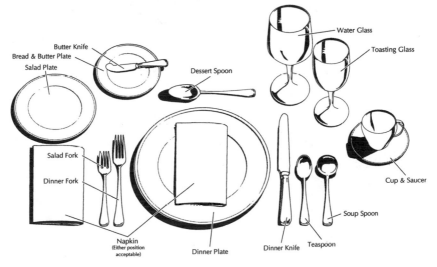

Figure 3.4
Utensil placement for the resting and closed positions.

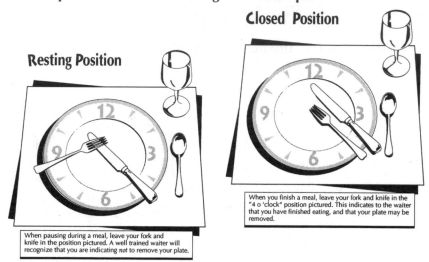

Resting Position

Closed Position

When pausing during a meal, leave your fork and knife in the position pictured. A well trained waiter will recognize that you are indicating *not* to remove your plate.

When you finish a meal, leave your fork and knife in the "4 o 'clock" position pictured. This indicates to the waiter that you have finished eating, and that your plate may be removed.

Figure 3.5
Illustration of the positions for holding utensils.

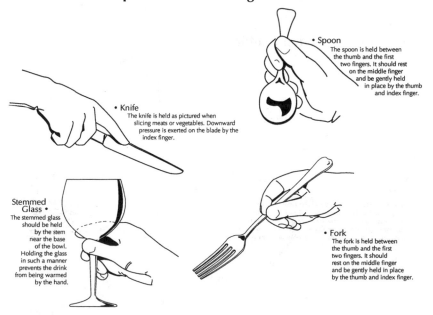

• Spoon
The spoon is held between the thumb and the first two fingers. It should rest on the middle finger and be gently held in place by the thumb and index finger.

• Knife
The knife is held as pictured when slicing meats or vegetables. Downward pressure is exerted on the blade by the index finger.

Stemmed Glass •
The stemmed glass should be held by the stem near the base of the bowl. Holding the glass in such a manner prevents the drink from being warmed by the hand.

• Fork
The fork is held between the thumb and the first two fingers. It should rest on the middle finger and be gently held in place by the thumb and index finger.

well-trained server will not have to interrupt your conversation to ask if you have finished. It is a subtle yet powerful way to signal the server that he may remove your plate. (See Figure 3.4.)

American and Continental Eating Styles

There are two basic eating styles: American and Continental. Choose your style, master it well, and use it consistently. (See Figures 3.5 and 3.6.) In the American style, commonly used in the United States, the knife and fork are held to cut several bites of food. The knife is placed on the plate, and the fork is rotated and transferred to the right hand. The American style is also known as *American Zig Zag*. In the Continental style, the knife and fork remain in the right and left hands respectively throughout the meal. The fork tines are always turned downwards. One piece of food is cut, pushed onto the fork, and lifted to the mouth. The knife remains in the right hand. The Continental style is more efficient. If you eat using the Continental style, be aware that the practicality of not having to transfer utensils enables you to eat quickly. Be attentive to keep your consumption pace equal to that of your tablemates.

Figure 3.6
Illustration of the Continental and American eating styles.

Two eating styles are **Continental & American**

American style: Utensils are lifted from the table with fork in the left hand, knife in the right. Hold the fork with the tines down. The index finger anchors the utensil by pointing toward the tines. Hold the knife with handle in palm, index finger pointing down the handle, anchoring the knife. After cutting two or three pieces of food, place the knife on the edge of the plate, transfer the fork to the right hand, rotate and lift to mouth with tines up.

Please avoid these improper handling of the dining utensils. You will appear clumsy and unprofessional and/or child-like.

Continental style: Food is cut the same as above description. Cut one piece at a time. Leave the utensils in the same hands, bring the fork to the mouth with the tines down. The knife remains in the right hand. Practice pushing food onto the back of the fork. This is quick and efficient so eat slowly. Observe your tablemates to pace your eating speed.

THE BUSINESS MEAL

At a business meal when do I discuss the business?
Serious business talk is saved for later in the meal after the entrée plates have been removed. By talking about other subjects, you avoid the problems of balancing fork in hand, food in mouth, and important conversation. Serious business conversation takes concentration. Save yourself for the important stuff and enjoy the meal and friendly conversation.

You have invited a guest to have a meal and discuss your proposal and contract. Conduct the meal by being a thoughtful hostess and performing your responsibilities as hostess. During the first course or two, you can talk about light business: how things are going at the office, how the job is going, business growth, and business outreach in the community. All of your conversation should lead to the important reason you called the business meal. You may gain valuable information to use in the context of your business or contract presentation. Being informed about a company gives you topics for conversation and insight as to the direction of the business. Conversation topics during the early part of the meal might also include vacation activities, sports, personal interests, or even your children (when appropriate).

You are always a representative of your company so you must be prepared to practice good table and business manners. The point of having good table manners is that when you know what to do you can be relaxed and enjoy the meal and the meeting. You will be flexible and comfortable because you have learned how to use the dining tools and manage the business meal effectively.

Seating order and table location are important considerations during business meetings (see Figure 3.7). You can be subtle about arranging these details. If you are the host, ask for a table in a well-lighted area away from the serving staff's path to the kitchen. The host should be seated facing away from the wall (and into the dining area) so that he can summon the server easily. Prior to seating, the host should decide the chair location for the guest. The location is deter-

Figure 3.7
Location for friendly conversation.

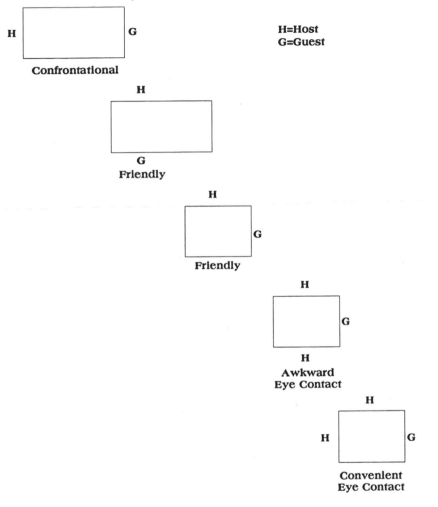

mined by the number of guests and hosts. You want the seating to be friendly, not confrontational, and comfortable, not stuffy, to facilitate easy conversation.

You can help the servers to serve you better by keeping the area around your chair free of handbags, briefcases, computers, and papers. Avoid hanging items off the back of your chair that might fall off and interfere with the server's work. Do thank the servers when they are attentive, and tip accordingly.

If you initiated the meal meeting, then you are considered the host. With hosting, you have responsibilities to

- ❖ Confirm the date and time with your guests in advance.
- ❖ Make a reservation.
- ❖ Arrive early to select the table and greet your guests.

The host has other responsibilities as well. To make the business meal a comfortable meeting, the host should make payment arrangements prior to being seated. By arriving early the host can leave the credit card with the maitre d' then sign for the charges when leaving the restaurant, thereby eliminating the whole confusion or awkwardness at the table of who pays. A guest feels at ease when greeted by the host upon arrival and being shown where to sit. The most important guest is seated to the right of the host; the second most important guest on the host's left. As the host you can prepare an agenda and provide copies of it to keep the business focus.

It is helpful to be familiar with the restaurant and the menu. You may make subtle, helpful suggestions from the menu if you are familiar with it: "The crab cakes and Caesar salad are always delicious" or "I frequently order the special of the day. It is always good." These suggestions ease the guest's uncertainty about what to order. It also indicates the meal budget and the number of courses and is an indication of the amount of time the host has allowed for the meeting. You might prefer to simply suggest to your guests that they order an appetizer, and soup or salad, with their entrée, and that you'll have dessert with your coffee or tea after the meal. An associate of mine always begins the meal by asking his guest if he would like an appetizer. It is his company's policy to encourage their guests to order whatever they wish, and this early offer helps to establish that fact.

May I order dessert?
The host should offer the option. Generally at lunch, dessert is not ordered, but at dinner when the meeting is longer, dessert may be ordered. It should only be done at the host's suggestion, not the guest's. The host sets the pace and number of courses at the meal.

The guest has responsibilities as well. The guest is expected to arrive on time, dressed appropriately, and prepared to discuss the agenda topics. The guest is attending a business meeting and should be prepared with information about the host and the company. He should carry business cards and company brochures; he may not need them, but he is better prepared for the unanticipated if he carries them. Both the host and the guest should know how to use the dining tools properly. In general, it is wise to avoid alcoholic beverages, but the guest may follow the host's lead. As a guest, you should take cues from your host's food suggestions. In fact, you may want to ask your host for menu suggestions, if none are given.

Use of the dinner napkin is often overlooked, but is important nonetheless. When you first sit down, place yourself at a distance from the table of about seven inches (your wrist to fingertips), and unfold the napkin and put it in your lap. Fold one edge of the napkin down two inches with fold toward your body. Use your napkin during the course of the meal to keep your fingers and mouth clean; dab your mouth often with the napkin. Frequent use of your napkin will help you to avoid unsightly greasy lip and finger marks on your glassware. The napkin is not a tissue for your nose.

Keep your napkin in your lap until you rise to leave the restaurant. If you leave the table, put your napkin in your chair until you return.

Practice good table manners while dining. Remember to use the utensils starting furthest from the plate. "Liquids on the right, solids on the left." Your bread and butter plate is on the left of your place setting, beverages are on the right. Your host will signal to "begin eating" by lifting his utensil.

As you eat, remember to swallow before speaking and chew with your lips closed. You will be more relaxed and better able to concentrate on your guests if you avoid stringy pasta, fried chicken, or slippery seafood dishes. Sit straight and keep your elbows off the table. Remember: "Elbows never, forearms sometimes, wrists always."

Men should keep their jackets on unless the local culture dictates otherwise. Some restaurants require that the jacket be worn during the meal. Neckties may be secured to the shirt underneath with a shirt-tie accessory; if you prefer not to use a tie tack or tie clip of some kind, take care not to let your tie fall into your plate. Neckties should not be tossed over the shoulder. Ladies may rotate their scarves so they won't fall into the soup.

You are at a business meal. Concentrate on the people you are dining with and the business you wish to conduct. Avoid moving from table to table to greet other friends or associates. Avoid conversation with another table as much as possible. Acknowledge your friends across the room with a nod and smile. When you turn off your cell phone, you send a message to your host or your guests that they and their time are important and that you respect them. Avoid using your cell phone at the table; excuse yourself from the table if you must make a call.

If you leave the table, push in your chair, and make the simple statement, "Please excuse me for a moment." Make the departure brief.

Gaffes at the Business Dining Table

- ❖ Getting too personal in conversation
- ❖ Complaining about business colleagues
- ❖ Finishing other's sentences
- ❖ Interrupting the conversation
- ❖ Using profanity or telling inappropriate jokes
- ❖ Starting the business conversation before the conclusion of the entrée
- ❖ Putting business papers on the table before business discussion begins
- ❖ Wearing inappropriate clothing
- ❖ Coughing without covering your mouth
- ❖ Burping

❖ Yawning

❖ Getting out a mirror at the table

The type of meeting and location must be considered if you plan a mixed gender meeting. Avoid breakfast and late dinner meetings when these might be misconstrued as romantic meetings.

Wine Etiquette

Avoid ordering alcoholic beverages. If you or your guests are representing the wine industry you might make an exception but, generally, it is preferable to avoid mixing business with alcohol consumption. Some corporations have a no-alcohol policy. Often there is a penalty for not following policy, so be sensitive about these restrictions with which you are unfamiliar.

If ordering wine is appropriate,

❖ Ask for suggestions from the server or wine steward.

❖ Sample the wine for flavor. In rare cases, you may refuse the wine because it is spoiled; however, you may not refuse if you do not like the taste.

❖ Do not smell the cork. Instead, pinch the cork for moisture.

The Four Types of Business Meals

There are four meals at which you may conduct a business meeting while dining: at breakfast, lunch, afternoon tea, and dinner. Table manners are a major part of any meeting that involves dining. Naturally, each has specific benefits related to time of day and length of meeting. Select the one that will best suit your purposes and situation.

Breakfast Meetings

❖ Can be brief (one hour).

❖ Commence at 6:00 or 7:00 A.M.

❖ Discourage alcohol consumption due to the early hour.

❖ Offer few business distractions because they begin before most people are at work.

❖ Leave the rest of the day open to complete additional business.

Lunch Meetings

* ❖ Occur in the middle of the day and generally last two to three hours.
* ❖ Commence between 11:00 and 1:00 P.M.
* ❖ Allow for preparation for the meeting in the morning.
* ❖ Allow afternoon time for follow-up.
* ❖ May be casual.

Afternoon Tea Meetings

* ❖ Begin after 3:00 P.M. and last one and a half to two hours.
* ❖ Discourage alcohol consumption.
* ❖ May be either casual or formal.
* ❖ Occur late enough to conclude the workday.
* ❖ Are generally less expensive than lunch.
* ❖ May serve as an early dinner.
* ❖ Are frequently memorable because they are different from the more usual breakfast, lunch, or dinner meetings.

Dinner Meetings

* ❖ May continue as late as 11:00 P.M. and are perhaps the longest of the meal meetings.
* ❖ Are generally more formal and may require more formal dress than worn at the office.
* ❖ May be initiated by written invitation.
* ❖ May include spouses or significant others.
* ❖ Can become a social event when nonbusiness guests such as spouses are included.

Power Tea

When lunch seems too long, or your expense budget is already stretched, try an afternoon or Power Tea. Tea is part of almost every culture in the world. Show yourself to be different, creative, and perhaps memorable by inviting someone to experience tea. Afternoon tea is served at tearooms and some hotels from 2:00 to 5:30 P.M., depending on the location. You may meet at a hotel lobby to share business conversation over a cup of tea and sandwiches. Try tea even if you are not normally a tea drinker. Taking afternoon tea at 3:00 or 4:00 P.M. is a sophisticated way to end the workday, meet a client, conduct business, interview a prospective employee, entertain clients, and/or enjoy a light meal.

There are several reasons for having tea (also known as taking tea) with a business colleague. Teatime occurs in the afternoon and enables you to spend at least three-quarters of the workday in the office. There are no questions about alcohol consumption; the beverage is tea. Generally, a tea meeting will be less expensive than a lunch meeting. You spend less time away from the office. The setting can be as comfortable or formal as you choose. The setting is usually spacious and well-lighted. Afternoon tea is memorable. It works well with mixed gender meetings, but be familiar with the location so that it does not convey a romantic setting.

Who pours the tea?

The host pours the tea for his guests. If there is more than one host, the junior host pours in respect to the others.

Power Tea Etiquette

- Be knowledgeable about the hotel/tearoom services.
- Make reservations in advance.
- Arrive early and select a well-lighted table.
- Arrange for payment in advance. Pay discreetly.
- Familiarize yourself with the menu.
- Learn the house specialties and tea terminology, for example, afternoon tea is a mini-meal while high tea is at 6:00 P.M.
- Arrange with the hotel to pay for your guest's parking.
- Walk your guest to the exit when leaving.

Meeting for Coffee

Going out for coffee or meeting somewhere out of the office for coffee is another popular way to meet with one or two others for short business meetings. In most areas there are a number of coffeehouses specializing in coffees of different types, cappuccinos, mochas, and lattes, as well as pastries.

Coffee establishments are often noisy and crowded, so they may not be suitable for all types of meetings. Coffee meetings are useful for keeping in touch with busy clients and developing or nurturing working relationships.

Many enjoy coffee at any time of day; some prefer coffee only in the morning. You may meet before work for a cup of coffee or later in the day. If you know your client enjoys coffee, surprise him by bringing his favorite to your morning meeting.

Gratuity Guide

A gratuity, or tip, is generally given as a gift above the cost of the service to the person who has provided the service. Restaurant servers, taxi cab drivers, and hairdressers/barbers are among the many people who are commonly offered a gratuity for their services. In the United States these individuals are frequently paid low or minimum wages and depend upon tips for a part of their income. You are not obligated to give a gratuity, but it is expected and appreciated, particularly if the server has provided good or excellent service to you and your party.

You appear more professional when you know the proper etiquette for gratuities, can tip without fuss, and are discreet about the amount of the tip. You may choose to leave a more generous gratuity if the service has been exceptional or you are a regular customer. Gratuities may vary in different geographic areas. For instance, you might expect to pay higher gratuities in New York City than you would in a small town in the Midwest. The following is only a guide and is not meant to be all-inclusive. Special situations may have their own set of gratuity guidelines.

WHEN YOU ARE THE HOST

In addition to the many host responsibilities mentioned earlier, the following also apply:

- ❖ Extend the invitation personally at least three days in advance.
- ❖ Be specific about the reason for the meeting.
- ❖ Be clear about where to meet (foyer, table, etc.).
- ❖ Stand when the guests arrive and shake hands.
- ❖ Keep conversation to light business until after the main course plate is cleared.

Gratuity Guide

Maître d'	$5.00–$20.00 if you are a regular at the restaurant or you have received extra service
Captain (of serving staff)	5% of the dinner tab
Restaurant server	15–20% of the dinner tab
Sommelier (wine steward)	$3.00–5.00/bottle or 15% of wine cost (given directly to the sommelier when the wine is opened at your table)
Bartender	15–20% of the bar tab
Restroom attendant	$ .50–1.00
Coat clerk	$1.00–2.00/coat
Parking valet (when you are leaving	$1.00–3.00
Doorman (when he hails a cab for you)	$1.00–2.00
Taxi cab driver	15% of the bill
Caterer	15–20% of the bill
Hotel maid	$1.00–1.50/day per person
Bellman or airport skycap	$1.00/bag
Concierge (for reservations, favors)	$2.00–20.00
Room service (service charge included on bill)	$1.00–5.00 (in addition to service charge)
Private club personnel	$50.00–100.00 donation to employee fund at holidays
Building doorman	$10.00–100.00 at holidays

❖ Delay your business discussion until coffee and dessert.

❖ Set a comfortable atmosphere.

❖ Ask questions to encourage conversation.

❖ Discuss important points of the business meeting before leaving the table.

❖ Signal the end of the meeting by placing your napkin on the table and rising from your chair.

Sometime your schedule may require a cancellation of a meal meeting. Everyone understands when the cancellation is done with consideration to the other person's schedule. If you need to cancel, do it with a personal call. There is no need to give a reason other than saying "I have a conflict in my schedule." If you are the host, reschedule the meeting when you call.

WHEN YOU ARE THE GUEST

- ❖ Confirm day and time if the invitation is made more than one week in advance.
- ❖ Arrive on time. If you cannot avoid being more than fifteen minutes late, phone the restaurant to advise your host when to expect you.
- ❖ The hostess may direct you to a seat. Wait for the hostess to ask you to be seated.
- ❖ Confine your conversation to business-related subjects.
- ❖ Follow your host's lead in ordering beverages.
- ❖ Let the host give menu suggestions. Order thoughtfully and be aware of costs.
- ❖ Set a comfortable atmosphere.
- ❖ Ask questions to encourage conversation.
- ❖ Be prepared to pay in the event that there was a misunderstanding of host roles.
- ❖ If you must cancel, call personally, apologize, and suggest a rescheduling.
- ❖ Send a thank you note after the meeting.

After the meeting is it appropriate to "talk business" in the restroom?
Yes. There is no rule that business discussion cannot be conducted in places other than at the meeting table. Confiden-

tiality is the most important factor. Be aware of others who might overhear. And be cognizant of any other persons who need to be part of the discussion.

Sometimes decisions are made more easily in a relaxed setting. That is why business entertaining at venues like country clubs is part of business etiquette knowledge. Get your manners mastered and the power of knowing what to do will follow you.

Awkward situations sometimes occur at business meetings. One afternoon a colleague telephoned to ask my opinion about a situation. He had been the guest of a woman for lunch. When the bill came, it was placed in front of him. As he looked at his host, she looked at the table, then excused herself to go to the rest room. She returned to the table after a lengthy absence but did not acknowledge the bill or offer to pay it. JR was left with the bill. He was perplexed and annoyed, but paid it. His call to me was to ask what he should have done. My response was to question him on whether he wanted to conduct business with her again. His answer was an emphatic "Yes." What would you do? These were his options. JR could have

- ❖ Pushed the bill across the table to her.
- ❖ Asked her if she was hosting this time.
- ❖ Suggested that they split the bill.
- ❖ Paid it and said nothing.

I suggested that the next time he meets her for a meal that he be very clear who is hosting. In most cases, the one who initiated the invitation is the host, and payment is the host's responsibility. It is also important for the host to inform the server that she is to receive the bill. Guests may not be prepared to pay with cash. You may choose to split the bill, but that needs to be decided at the time of ordering. Sometimes the server will agree to write separate bills or will total each guest's charge and circle it. Sometimes the establishment will allow a bill to be split evenly and charged equally to two charge cards. These options should also be arranged with the server in advance, preferably at the time of ordering. Always carry cash so you will be prepared for whatever unforeseen situation might arise. If one bill arrives for more than two people, the general rule is to divide it evenly among the number of people. Yes, there are those who order more expensive courses and more courses than others, but the easiest way is to divide the amount evenly. Next time you dine out, you will know how to order and with whom to dine!

What do you do when you agree to split the bill and the money collected does not add up to the total (plus the tip)? Someone has to add more money and it can be a sizable amount if the bill is large. I recently dined with sixteen people. We agreed that each person would contribute their portion according to what was ordered plus a specified amount for tax and tip. The money was $40 short of the total. Who didn't pay? Everyone contributed, but most likely every person undercalculated his portion and we had to collect an additional $2.50 from everyone to make up the deficit. Who pays? If you are the organizer, you may have to add extra. Another round of conversation will often bring a few dollars more, but then you must add the rest. If you choose to split the bill in this way, be prepared because often you'll come up short and have to make up the difference somehow!

TOASTS AND ROASTS

Toasts are always appropriate to acknowledge the occasion. If you are hosting a dinner party or entertaining foreign guests, be prepared with a toast or designate someone to make a toast. A toast is a compliment and acknowledgment of the event and guests. A toast is not about past events, people who are not present, or future achievements.

When a toast is given in honor of a guest, that person does not sip. The other guests sip after the toast and the toaster has sipped. The honored guest nods in respect. You do not drink to your own toast; it would be as though you were patting yourself on the back.

A toast might be as simple as "We are honored to have you, Mr. Guest, with us for this occasion of celebrating the completion of our project together." The guest in turn may reciprocate with his own toast. A toast is not the time to make your oratory about your philosophy of business. Save those comments for another time.

A roast, on the other hand, is a time to tell stories about your friends. Generally, roasts are offered at retirement celebrations, honoring celebrations, and birthday parties. The host should ask some of the guests prior to the event if they would like to roast. They can be prepared with their story. Some roasts are lengthy but there is no set time limit for a roast. The host may have to intervene if the oratory lasts longer than fifteen minutes.

Chapter 4

Write It Right

Υour clients measure the quality of your products and services by the image you project in your personal manners, appearance, words, and actions. Your printed business materials are equally important. Building a strong identity is vital to the success of your business. Your professional identity begins with the image created by your business communications. Visually pleasing, informational communication is essential for good business.

Frequently, you will make your first impression on potential clients with your advertising materials, your promotional literature, and your business stationery. A consistent business image is critical to your success. When your clients recognize your business, your business will increase. Your professional stationery ensemble consists of business cards, letterhead, envelopes, brochures, and any other printed material. They are a reflection of you and your business. The larger or more diverse the business becomes the more extensive the stationery ensemble will become.

Your paper image is your business identity. Like your business card, the stationery on which you write your letters, memos, or any correspondence is a reflection of you and how you conduct business. Consider how others will "see" or perceive you when they cannot speak personally with you or see you. How do you want people to respond when they open the letter or even see the envelope when it is delivered? What do you consider important as a visual message?

To develop a logo choose a design that projects who you are and what you do, something that will be easily identified or remembered. A logo can be the way you sign your name, your initials formed into a design, a drawing or illustration, or a meaningful symbol. Select a color that complements the business you are in or appeals to the type of clients you wish to attract. It is best to work with a graphic designer who can interpret what you are trying to say in graphics. If you are in business for yourself or just starting out, you may struggle with just how to position yourself visually. For some of us, it is a continual process. For those who work for a corporation that has an established logo, follow corporate policy on consistent usage of the logo, corporate name, and corporate stationery. E-mail and other electronic communications will be discussed in Chapter 5, Electronic Communication.

IMAGE OF BUSINESS COMMUNICATIONS

When developing your professional business stationery you will have a number of decisions to make. Most business people consult with a graphic designer or other similar professionals for assistance with this process. Some entrepreneurs invest in software to help them do-it-yourself. There are also preprinted, coordinated business papers that can be customized using your laser printer. Many of these entrepreneurs do just fine, others have no idea how bad their designs are for their business. Many people choose the do-it-yourself route, at least in the beginning, because it is cost effective (not to mention fun). If you choose to do-it-yourself, ask some colleagues for their honest opinion of your designs before you distribute them. Among other design considerations, you will need to consider the following:

- ❖ Quality, color, and texture of the paper
  The same paper will normally be used for your letterhead, envelopes, and business cards. It may also be used for other documents as well. If you plan to use the paper in your laser or inkjet printer, be aware that heavy weight and heavy textured paper stocks may not work well. Discuss this concern with your printer and/or graphics designer in advance.
- ❖ Design of the logo, symbol, or trademark of your business
  You may also have a slogan or phrase that will be used on your documents.

❖ Types of stationery you will need to conduct your business

❖ Ink color for printing the stationery

Sometimes foils are used for special effects, as are different types of lettering processes (defined below).

❖ Paper sizes for different documents

In general, letterhead is the standard 8½ x 11 inch with standard No. 10 business envelopes. You may want different-size papers for other applications.

❖ Typeface and size

Decisions on appropriate typeface and size are normally made in the process of developing the logo and designing business documents.

Ink color of the printed text and your ink pen should coordinate with the paper. Conservative and traditional businesses continue to prefer blue or black ink. Some professions reflect current trends and have more latitude in their business expression. These include the fashion, communication, and public relations industries. The ink choices for these organizations may include brighter or trendier colors. It is important to consider the reader's ability to read the print; make certain there is adequate contrast between your ink and paper colors. For instance, yellow text on white paper is difficult to read because there isn't enough contrast between yellow and white.

Small business people may design and print their own materials using their computers and laser printers. The professional printing/lettering process can be one of the following:

❖ Printing is most commonly used and is always appropriate for business cards, note cards, letterhead, and any other business documents.

❖ Thermography is a heat process causing ink to rise and gives an engraved feeling. It is common for business cards because it gives a richer feel to an inexpensive document.

❖ Engraving is expensive and requires a special steel die. It is used for very formal invitations and sometimes for upper management's stationery.

❖ Embossing is a bumped engraving that adds a special feeling of luxury. It is often used for invitations.

YOUR STATIONERY ENSEMBLE

Your initial professional stationery ensemble should include

❖ Letterhead paper, second sheets, and envelopes

❖ Business cards

❖ Business forms necessary to conduct business, for example, invoices, order forms, price sheets

❖ Informal or folded notes. These are not the same as note/enclosure cards but they could be used interchangeably until you have both kinds of note cards.

As you are promoted, your responsibilities increase, or your company grows, you will need additional stationery that may include social business cards (which are not the same as standard business cards), personalized memo pads, postcards or "keep-in-touch" cards (a postcard size on card stock with envelope), and perhaps small give-away items with your logo and name.

When you initially order your stationery, it is practical to print only what you are currently using or think that you will use in a reasonable period of time. You may not need as extensive a paper ensemble as listed above when you print your first materials. As you use the stationery, you will quickly learn what you really need and what you want to add in the next printing.

Letterhead and Envelopes

For letterhead, you may wish to use a design with basic information (address, phone) that can be used for different purposes. This is practical because of its versatility; you can use the same printed sheets for your letterhead, invoices, proposals, and other promotional sheets. The sheets are professionally printed. You can also use these sheets on your computer to print personalized materials for clients. The practicality of this piece is that you can save on professional printing costs. Rather than paying to print small quantities of several types of documents, you can print a larger quantity of one document that has multiple uses, and thus take advantage of quantity price breaks in printing. Your business envelopes are normally of the same paper stock as your letterhead.

Business Cards

Business cards often leave the first and most lasting impression of you and your business on the recipient. A business card is the first graphic statement we make about ourselves and our business when we hand them to others. Your business card is the handshake you leave behind. When someone looks at your card a few days or years after they met you they may not remember your face or what you said, but your card reminds them of you. Make certain it speaks with a smile and conjures good thoughts. Business cards are tools to remind a person of your connection with them, to keep in touch, to call back, or to conduct business with in the future. You never know where your cards will be five years from now.

Business cards should have essential information easily visible on the face of the card. Unless your company policy has a standardized format for corporate business cards that dictates otherwise, your name should be large and prominent. If someone calls and reminds you of a conversation a few years prior that you have forgotten, you can be assured that they liked your card and made some notes about you on it.

It is not necessary to leave the card back blank. You may use the space on the back for product listing, services offered, a map to your location, or an interesting quote. Keep the back simple and uncluttered. If you work with clients who do not speak English, you may wish to have the back of your card printed in the second language. Be sure to include your name and your title in the second language, along with your phone number.

Your business cards should include

❖ Your name and title, if any
❖ Company name and logo

❖ Business address

❖ Telephone and fax number

❖ E-mail address and web site address, if any

❖ Addresses of other offices in the country (if applicable)

Many people use electronic contact management programs and may scan your card into a computer database. Others may keep the cards in a box or file. Your card is the story you leave behind. If the memory is positive and meaningful, the card is often used for future contact. Your business card and how you use it are an important part of your communication. You should use your cards in such a way that the recipient will want to contact you again.

Your business cards may be used in many ways. Normally, cards are used to introduce you and your business and as a reminder of who you are and where you can be reached. Business cards may also be included as a forwarding agent when attached to a report, newspaper clipping, photograph, or something you promised to send. Some business cards are even used as an enclosure for a gift or flowers (although a social card is preferable). Include a business card in correspondence when it seems appropriate. It is nice to be remembered; make sure your business card helps you to be remembered favorably.

❖ Your business cards should be clean, with no bent or curled edges.

❖ All the information on your card should be current.

❖ The card design should be interesting with effective use of white space. White space is the space where there is nothing printed. Adequate white space gives a clean, professional look rather than an amateur one. Don't crowd your business card with text.

❖ Your card may include a company or business logo, as well as an affiliation or association logo, when appropriate. I use the NSA logo on mine to indicate that I am a member of the National Speakers Association. Corporate policy may not encourage use of this type of logo; check before you print cards.

Social Business Cards

Social business cards (also known as social cards) are the same size as standard business cards (3½ by 2 inches). Social cards are less frequently seen, but are useful. One may include them as gift or correspondence enclosures. Social business cards include only your full name in the center (generally without titles) and your telephone number at the lower right corner. Today's modern business person might print their full name in the center and their e-mail address and telephone number in the lower right corner. The design of the social business card leaves plenty of blank space for a greeting to be written on the face or on the back of the card. There may be times when you only wish to give your social business card. When you meet a colleague you wish to maintain contact with, but do not want to appear strictly business, use your social card. It serves the same purpose without the commercialism of a business card.

Special Stationery

You can be creative with some of your stationery. One size that I personally like is printed "three up" on an 8½- by 11-inch sheet of card stock, trimmed to 8½ by 3⅔ inches. Each card fits nicely into a No. 10 envelope. My full name is printed across the top of each of the three pieces. I use them as personal notes, informal notes, and enclosures. The nature of your business may dictate how creative or conservative you may be in designing and using your stationery. Be sure your documents leave the professional impression so crucial to your success.

Business Announcements

Announcements inform clients about changes in your business: a new address, a new partner, an appointment, a promotion, or the introduction of a new product or service. They have more impact than a telephone call or a statement made in conversation. Avoid crowding the visual impact of the card with too much information. The design should be attractive and should invite the recipient to read it. The recipient may call for more details, and you may be able to use the opportunity to make a new contact or sale.

A formal announcement is printed with just the facts and is sent in an envelope. The envelopes are most effective when they are handwritten because the handwriting implies a personal touch and thereby increases the likelihood the envelope will be opened rather than thrown away. Announcements should be printed on high-quality white or ecru (off-white) paper. If you wish to use some other color paper or print a postcard instead, be careful when an announcement is printed on one sheet of bright paper or as a postcard, there is some risk that it will be perceived as unimportant because it looks like a sales flyer. The typeface used for your announcement should be in an easily readable style in either black or another dark-color ink. Handwritten notes are often included to further personalize the announcement. Announcements do not require an acknowledgment from the recipient, but it is a courteous gesture to send a note of congratulation if one is in order.

LETTER WRITING

Letter writing has become a lost art. It is, nonetheless, an important part of business and personal communications. Be sure to open your correspondence promptly and respond accordingly. Your handwritten letter or thank you note may be a surprise to the recipient, will be greatly appreciated, and may even be framed for the wall! Any time that you have an opportunity to make a personal contact, it has significance and impact on building the relationship and your credibility.

Business letters are communication tools for daily business and are typed. Personal correspondence and personal business are handwritten unless, of course, your handwriting is illegible! If you prefer to type your personal letter, add a handwritten line or two at the bottom.

Your style of expressing concern and interest in others will be evident in your correspondence. Before anyone reads a word of your letter or note, you have made an impression. The information the letter contains may be lost if the visual presentation is not well received. The text of business letters must be well placed on the stationery. Avoid using whiteout to correct spelling errors and misprinting. Use correct English to communicate your ideas.

Correspondence of any form has guidelines and rules. Correct spelling and good grammar are expected. Complete sentences, accurate word choice, correct sentence structure, and punctuation are essential to conveying both your message and your professionalism. Use of proper salutations, appropriate names, and proper letterform are important.

Before you begin any written correspondence you will need the recipient's correctly spelled name and address. A letter with the name misspelled leaves the immediate impression that the sender doesn't know the recipient, doesn't pay attention to details, or doesn't care if they leave a poor impression. We draw conclusions based on what we learn from many sources, including correspondence and other business materials. Take the time and effort to spell and pronounce peoples' names correctly. One's name is the most precious sound in any language.

When preparing to write a letter, telephone the company even if it is long distance to confirm the person's correct name, spelling, and any appropriate title. Using the person's name personalizes the letter. The salutation should simply be "Dear Mr. Green" or "Dear Ms. Green." Use a colon (:) as punctuation following the salutation if you do not personally know the addressee, a comma (,) if you do. The closure may read "Sincerely," "Cordially," or "Regards." A more formal closure is used for international correspondence, such as "Very truly yours," "Very sincerely," or "Respectfully yours." International closures are more formal than contemporary American style and are important to use in business correspondence.

There are two generally accepted letter writing forms: block and modified block. The block form requires the date, recipient's address, salutation, body of letter, and closure to all align on the left margin (flush left or left justified). The first lines of paragraphs are not indented in block form letters. Modified block form allows for the parts of the letter to be indented. A sample of each form follows. The sample business letters would be typed on preprinted letterhead that would already include the sender's name, company, and corporate address and telephone.

Either block or modified block form may be used. Master one well and use it for all your correspondence. Using the same letterform for all your business correspondence helps to establish your image, just as your letterhead and logo do. The basics for letter writing are simple and consistency is important.

23 November 2009

Marguerite Daisy
Director of Public Relations
Bulbs, Incorporated
543 Flower Lane Suite 101
Garden City, CA 90000-1111

Dear Ms. Daisy,

This letter is an example of "block" form. In the block form all margins are left justified. Each paragraph has a blank line between, but has no indentation of the first line.

There is also a blank line between the addressee and the greeting/salutation and a blank line between the text and the closure. Your closure may be "Sincerely" or "Cordially." There are generally three blank lines between the closure and your typed name. This allows space for your signature above your typed name.

If there is an enclosure, indicate that under your name as "enclosure or enc."

Cordially,

Dana May Casperson
enclosure

When using the computer you may choose to use left justification or full justification (aligning both the right and left edges of the type). Business correspondence is generally done on a computer, so the text can be left or full justified.

Some like full justification, others prefer left justified/ragged right. Although the word spacing may be irregular in full justification, some people like the overall even look. Justified text was the style for many years, however, studies on readability show that the inconsistent spacing between the words inhibit the flow of reading. Be aware that when you choose full justification, you choose that look and sacrifice the most

---

23 November 2009

Marguerite Daisy
Director of Public Relations
Bulbs, Incorporated
543 Flower Lane Suite 101
Garden City, CA 90000-1111

Dear Ms. Daisy,

This letter is an example of "modified block" form. In the modified block form, indentation is allowed. Each paragraph has a blank line in between, and the first line of the paragraph is indented from the left margin.

There is also a blank line between the addressee and the greeting/salutation and a blank line between the text and the closure. The closure is indented from the left margin. There are generally three blank lines between the closure and your typed name. This allows space for your signature above your typed name.

If there is an enclosure, indicate that under your name as "enclosure or enc."

Cordially,

Dana May Casperson
enclosure

---

effective word spacing. Perhaps letters are best "left justified" since they are generally short and will look less like a form letter. The subtle details are the ones that leave the lasting impression!

Letters should express your personality and style yet conform to traditional letterforms. The most common errors are in the placement of the addressee, that is, the person to whom the letter is addressed and their mailing address, the greeting or salutation, and the closure or signature.

This is a sample of a **left-justified** (ragged right) paragraph. The left edge of the text is aligned, the right edge is not. The right edge is known as "ragged." Each of these sample paragraphs has the same left and right margin.	This is a sample of a **justified** paragraph. Both the right and left edges of the text align. To full justify the computer adjusts the space between words and letters, resulting in irregular spaces between the words.
A paragraph of the same words will demonstrate the difference between the look of a left justified and a fully justified paragraph.	A paragraph of the same words will demonstrate the difference between the look of a left justified and a fully justified paragraph.

- ❖ The inside address at the top of the letter should include the addressee's name followed by their job title, the full name of the company, the company address and postal code.

- ❖ Your closure and signature should match the formality of the greeting.

- ❖ Your full name and any title should always be typed after the closure with enough space between the closure and your name for your signature.

- ❖ You may sign with your first name when your full name is printed. Using just your first name lends an air of informality; be sure this is your intention.

- ❖ If additional material is included with the letter, the word "enclosure" under your typed name is sufficient.

- ❖ An informal business letter follows the same format, except that the salutation includes the first name or the first and last name rather than the title followed only by the last name. "Dear Bob" or "Dear Bob Smith" would be used rather than "Dear Mr. Smith."

If you have not composed letters for a while, begin now. The more practice you have, the more proficient and confident you will become.

Formal language indicates a formality that may not represent who you are. The form of your letter, your word choice, and your sentence structure make your letter formal or informal. There is a distinction between informal and incorrect!

There is a big difference between conversation and writing. The purpose of writing is communication, hence it should be simple enough to be understood readily, much as conversation should be. Your writing style should reflect your conversational style in that it should be easy to understand. Conversation may be riddled with incomplete sentences and grammar you would never use in your writing. Listen to one side of a telephone conversation to hear what I mean. This is acceptable in conversation because the person you are communicating with is participating in the conversation. You both have opportunity to make or ask for clarification of what is said. Written communication must be clear from the outset, without overuse of jargon or $50 words that obscure rather than clarify your meaning. Good writing is not necessarily formal writing; it may be friendly and conversational.

> ### Why does it matter how I form my letter?
> Your attention to detail, neatness, clarity of written word, and effort are unspoken examples of your professionalism and competence. Your letter is a reflection of your values and how you conduct business. The more your potential client knows about you, the better he can make his decision about whether he wants to pursue a business relationship with you. In addition, your client observes your skills and your personality through your correspondence.

State the purpose of your letter in the first paragraph. As you write your letter, do not use slang or expletives; keep jargon and acronyms to a minimum. Your purpose is to communicate, not confuse. Keep your writing to one page, if possible. Be concise.

Whether writing a letter, a note of acknowledgment, request, inquiry, thank you, or other business correspondence, you have the opportunity to make a lasting impression. Give a moment of thought to how the recipient may perceive you.

If you cannot spell well, use a spell checker, dictionary, thesaurus, and business correspondence guidebook to make your letters and correspondence look professional and credible. Computer spell checkers and grammar checkers can save you endless amounts of time and help you to be concise, professional, and make a positive impression.

The Date Form

In the United States, the date is routinely written with the month first, followed by the day and year, that is, Month DD, YYYY or MM/DD/YY (where M is month, D is day, and Y is year). We are accustomed to seeing dates in the form July 4, 2009.

In Europe, the accepted form for the date places the day first, as the most important part of the date, followed by the month and year, that is, DD Month YYYY or DD/MM/YY. This is the accepted international date form. Imagine the confusion if the date, July 4, 2009, was written 7/4/09 to a European colleague who would read the date as 7 April 2009. If you do any international business, consider using the international form of the date, where the day is written before the month and year. The international form of the date is used in the examples in this book.

WRITING A NOTE

Frequently, it will be more appropriate to send a note than a letter. In general, notes are much briefer and less formal than letters and may be written for a variety of different purposes and occasions. An informal handwritten note may use first names in the salutation, have indented paragraphs, and have the date, closure, and signature on the right. A note may be written

- ❖ As an informal invitation.
- ❖ As a reply to a written invitation.
- ❖ To thank someone for a gift.
- ❖ To offer condolences to a friend or associate.
- ❖ As a thoughtful and gracious gesture after lunch, dinner, or meeting.

❖ To congratulate a colleague on an honor, promotion, award, or job well done.

❖ To acknowledge the marriage, birth, graduation, or other milestone of a business associate or a member of his family.

❖ To follow-up after an appointment.

❖ To follow-up and thank the interviewer after a job interview.

❖ To offer an apology.

❖ As an acknowledgment or thank you after sharing a business lunch or tea.

For personal notes, only the first and last names are necessary. For professional appearance, avoid abbreviations, such as Dir. of PR (Director of Public Relations).

Writing a Thank You Note

In our fast-paced world, people often think that a verbal thank you is enough. It is not. A written note of thanks is an expression of courtesy whether written to a friend or a business associate. Follow-up with a written note; it will set you apart from others. You can never be assured that the voice message, fax, or even e-mail was received and read by the intended individual.

                                                          Date

Salutation,

   The first sentence should include a statement of appreciation and a thank you. The second sentence should acknowledge the event.

   The third sentence should make a comment about future contacts. Leave a blank line before the closure.

                                                    Closure,

                                                    Signature

---

A written note is a gentle gesture of kindness. When you write a thank you note, you need only write three sentences. One, to express thanks for a specific event or occasion, second, to acknowledge the event, and third, to make a statement about a future meeting or comment about the other person's success. If possible, avoid beginning your note with "I" or "Thank you." The sample below is done in modified block form. It takes only a few minutes to write and has a big impact on the receiver.

Thank you notes can be as simple or elaborate as you choose. They should express your personal style, and they should be handwritten, not typed. Keep note cards, matching envelopes, and postage stamps on hand (see Your Stationery Ensemble, earlier in this chapter) so that you will be able to write the cards within five days of the event.

A letter or note expressing gratitude for company hospitality should be sent on your company stationery. It should be handwritten and signed by you rather than by your secretary or assistant.

To prevent my own writing procrastination, I address the envelope and stamp it. When I see it on my desk, I do not want to waste a stamp and an envelope. It encourages me to write and mail the note.

---

25 November 2009

Dear Jennifer,

Our lunch together last Tuesday was fun. I appreciate your input on my project focus. Thanks for your suggestions about the proposal wording. I am always inspired by your enthusiasm!

I look forward to seeing you next month at the Connections meeting.

Best regards,

Dana May

---

30 July 2009

Dear Mr. Smith,

We appreciated your kind invitation to the holiday open house at your new office. The new location is a refreshing way to start the next tax season.

Steve and I enjoyed the event. We look forward to seeing you again soon. Our best wishes for success to your entire staff.

Best regards,

Dana May

Writing a Note of Condolence

A condolence note is an expression of sympathy on the death of someone. You need only express your personal concern in a few sentences in a handwritten note. If you prefer, you may add a handwritten note to a condolence card. Remember that it is the thought that's important.

5 September 2009

Dear Mary,

Recently I learned of the death of your father. I offer you my sincerest sympathy on your loss.

I look forward to seeing you in the very near future on your next trip to New York. If I can help you in any way, please call.

Best regards,

Dana May

The proceeding examples simulate handwritten notes and illustrate how your message might look. Writing your notes by hand is always the first choice. A number of readily available computer typefaces (fonts) simulate handwriting. You might consider using a "handwriting" typeface for informal notes to appropriate contacts you meet. In this manner, you could continually and efficiently expand your circle of contacts. With a change of salutation and a bit of personalization, this "handwritten" note is ready to mail. You might "mail merge" a letter or note to multiple clients.

Instead of typing and sending "canned" letters to family, friends, and business associates, a friend of mine uses a handwriting typeface when she composes a basic letter. She adds a personal salutation, writes a unique beginning and ending, and another personal "handwritten" letter is ready to make someone feel special. Seasonal greetings are perfect for this approach.

Fancy and cursive style type fonts are useful for some purposes. They tend to be casual, friendly, and fun. Beware: these typefaces can undermine your professional message! Some choices are too abstract or difficult to read to be used for text. Save these for "fun" projects rather than business.

Writing Seasonal Notes and Greeting Cards

During the winter solstice most cultures have a celebration. It is an appropriate time to send holiday greetings. The selection of a card with a warm greeting of the season without religious messages are always appropriate. The sending of the card is an expression of consideration and serves to keep in touch. If you send any religious cards, be sure they complement the recipient's beliefs. Your sensitivity to personal beliefs shows your consideration and respect of others.

Frequently, seasonal cards are preprinted with your full name or the name of the business. If the first names of husband and wife are printed on the inside card, the wife's should be first. "Cindy West and Jerry Night" is correct if the wife uses a different surname, "Cindy and Jerry Night" if the wife uses her husband's name.

Corporate cards are normally printed with the name of the firm, not the president or owner. This practice facilitates use of the cards by different individuals in the firm or by the firm in general. To these cards, add a personal note or greeting signed with your first name.

Holiday greetings are a thoughtful way to keep in touch with business contacts, to express your appreciation for their business, and to remind them of your services. Any season of the year is appropriate to keep in touch. In fact, using the four seasons as a time to keep in touch is not only creative, but also thoughtful and appreciated. Winter is the most common season to send greetings, but the other three should not be overlooked. Seasonal greetings are a perfect time to personalize a basic letter and send to all those you wish to contact.

Addressing Envelopes

Business and social correspondence should include the titles Mr., Mrs., Ms., or Dr. A social invitation or correspondence would be directed to Mr. and Mrs. Jerry Night even if the woman used a surname other than her husband's or a hyphenated name. When the correspondence is a business one and both husband and wife are partners in the same business, the address form for the inside letter should read:

> Ms. Cindy West
> Mr. Jerry Night
> 1324 Clovis Dr Suite 140
> San Francisco CA 90000-1111

Follow the letter form for addressing envelopes. The lines are directly under one another. Most word processing programs can print a postal bar code that speeds the sorting process.

The address on the envelope should appear as follows:

> MS CINDY WEST
> MR JERRY NIGHT
> 1324 CLOVIS DR STE 140
> SAN FRANCISCO CA 90000-1111

Note that there is no punctuation in the address. The postal service prefers all capital letters and standard abbreviations, hand printed or typed using a standard typeface rather than a fancy one like script. The envelope address should be typed in all capital letters. Omit punctuation in the address: omit the periods on Ms. and Mr. and abbreviate Suite to STE or use the number (#) symbol. There should be no commas after the city and no period after the state. Use only the standard two capital letter abbreviation for the state. The post office reads the address from the bottom up so the most critical parts of the address should be ordered accordingly. The address won't look as elegant as on the letter itself, but it will speed through the post office's automated sorting equipment and may reach its destination sooner. The post office offers a free publication with addressing information.

In Addressing Envelopes

- ❖ Use full names and titles.
- ❖ Remember that handwritten envelopes are more personal even if the card has a preprinted name inside.
- ❖ Avoid using labels when possible, as they may be perceived as impersonal and your envelope may be left unopened.
- ❖ Be sure to include a return address in the upper left corner or on the back flap of the envelope. The recipient may not have your address or the post office may need the return address if the envelope is misaddressed.

In addressing correspondence, as in making introductions, knowing which individual to mention first and how to address husband and wife correctly is an important aspect of proper etiquette. When addressing correspondence to a business remember the following:

- ❖ If there are two business partners, list the one with greater seniority first, without consideration of gender.
- ❖ Correspondence should only be addressed to the person associated with the business, not to Mr. and Mrs. when Mrs. does not work at the office.

When addressing social correspondence from a business to a residence:

❖ Correspondence sent to the residence should be addressed to both Mr. and Mrs., even if you only know one.

❖ If the couple have separate names, use two lines to list both, with titles. List the man's name first.

❖ If the envelope is directed to two people of the same gender, list the person you know first.

PERSONAL AND PROFESSIONAL TITLES

The proper use of titles is an important part of social and business etiquette. Always use a title such as Mr., Mrs., or Ms. when addressing mail unless the individual has another title such as Dr. Professional titles are used after the individual's name. If a person has written a title after the name, use it in your correspondence to them. Use the professional title and omit the Ms. or Mr.

Herb Brosbe, M.D.	*not*	Dr. Herb Brosbe, M.D.
Marion Jones, R.S.C.J.	*not*	Sister Marion Jones, R.S.C.J.
Patricia Steel, R.N.	*not*	Ms. Patricia Steel, R.N.
Lynn Smith, Ph.D.	*not*	Dr. Lynn Smith, Ph.D.

In business there is no marital distinction for women; the preferred title is Ms. If a woman signs her letters with Mrs. she has indicated she wants to be addressed as Mrs. In general, Ms. is the accepted title for a woman in business. For business correspondence, a woman is Ms. Jennifer Smith, not Mrs. Jennifer Smith (unless she has indicted she wants to be addressed as Mrs. or is an elderly widow). She should be addressed as Mrs. John Smith for social purposes.

Use the title for business correspondence when you know it:

Ms. Jennifer Newman
Vice President, Company Name
[Mailing address
City State Zip]

The title, Dr., refers to an MD (Medical Doctor), Ph.D. (Doctor of Philosophy), DVM (Doctor of Veterinary Medicine), DDS (Doctor of Dental Science), and honorary doctor. Use either the title (never spelled out) *or* degree letters but not both.

Dr. Linda Jones or
Linda Jones, Ph.D.,   *not*   Dr. Linda Jones, Ph.D.

Linda Jones, Ph.D.
[Company Name
Mailing address
City State Zip]

The title that follows the name designates a generational title such as Jr., Sr., or III. Jr. indicates the son has the same name as his father; the father may use Sr. when his son has the same name. When the father dies, the son may drop the Jr. from his name. If the Jr. gives his son the same name, the son uses the generational title III (the 3rd), that is, Matthew Newman III. A son given the exact name of a grandfather or uncle becomes II (the 2nd). Use these titles only when using the full name; follow the name with a comma before the title except for II, III, and IV and a period after the title except for II, III and IV: Mr. John H. Smith, Jr., and Mr. William B. Jones III.

Esquire (Esq.) is a chosen title reserved for attorneys. J.D., Doctor of Jurisprudence, is also used. Esq. is used only in professional or business correspondence.

Holly Rickett, J.D. or
Holly Rickett, Esq.   *not*   Ms. Holly Rickett, Esq.

Holly Rickett, Esq.
[Company Name
Mailing address]

Avoid abbreviating business titles as much as possible; Director of Public Relations looks much more professional (and respectful) than Dir. of PR.

Invitations are considered social so require a slightly different etiquette protocol.

When addressing the invitation to husband and wife:

Mr. and Mrs. Jerry Night
[*Home address*]

Or, when Mrs. uses a professional name:

Mr. Jerry Night and Ms. Cindy West
[*Home address*]

Or, when Mrs. has a title and Mr. does not

Mr. Jerry Night and Dr. Cindy West
[*Home address*]

Or, when both have same title

Dr. Jerry Night and Dr. Cindy West
[*Home address*]

or

The Doctors Night
[*Home address*]

In Europe much more importance is attached to titles than here in the United States. Europeans take great pride in receiving and in using their titles. When addressing foreign business persons, be certain you know their titles and use them in correspondence and when speaking.

WRITING AIDS

At the place where you write your letters, you will need a dictionary and thesaurus. These aids exist in word processing but there are times when a more extensive reference is needed. It adds to your efficiency to have reference books that you can scan for more precise information.

Having your supplies easily accessible makes the task of letter writing easier. Supplies need to be visible on your desk. Invest in good writing materials. Purchase fine quality paper for your stationery, a well-designed letterhead, and envelopes that match and are the appropriate

Title	Introductions / Envelopes	Salutation	Speaking to	Place Card
Clergyman	The Reverend John Hopkins *socially:* The Reverend and Mrs. John Hopkins	Dear Mr. Hopkins	Reverend *or* Mr. Hopkins	Mr. Hopkins
Clergywoman	The Reverend Lynn Newman *socially:* The Reverend Lynn Newman and Mr. Chris Jones	Ms. Newman	Reverend *or* Ms. Newman	Ms. Newman
Priest	The Reverend Father Matt Smith	Dear Father Smith	Father	Father Smith
Nun	Sister Marion	Dear Sister	Sister	Sister Marion
Rabbi	Rabbi Jacob Stein *socially:* Rabbi and Mrs. Jacob Stein	Dear Rabbi Stein	Rabbi	Rabbi Stein

Title	Introductions / Envelopes	Salutation	Speaking to	Place Card
The President of the United States	The President The White House	Dear Mr. President	Mr. President	The President
The First Lady	Mrs. Washington *socially:* The President and Mrs. Washington	Dear Mrs. Washington	Mrs. Washington	Mrs. Washington
U.S. Senator	The Honorable Diane Wise	Dear Senator Wise	Senator *or* Senator Wise	Senator Wise
Governor	The Honorable Matt Smith	Dear Governor *or* Dear Governor Smith	Governor *or* Governor Smith	Governor of California
State Senator	The Honorable Lynn Jones	Dear Senator Jones	Senator Jones	Senator Jones
Mayor	The Honorable Jerry Night	Dear Mr. Mayor *or* Dear Mayor Night	Mayor Night	The Mayor of Santa Rosa
Judge	The Honorable Robert Rivers	Dear Judge Rivers	Judge Rivers	Judge Rivers

size. Your pen should be a good-quality fountain pen (keep a supply of ink refills or ink bottle handy), a rollerball style pen, or a ballpoint pen.

Proofread your letters: spell check and grammar check them. If your letter is composed on the computer this can be done using the spell check function, though you should still proofread it. The spell check function will not catch words that are used incorrectly or spelled correctly. For instance, *"Merry hat hey lid tell lam, ids fleas woes wide has know"* is spelled perfectly but the message is totally missing: Mary had a little lamb, its fleece was white as snow. Only proofreading will catch these kinds of spelling and word errors. If you have difficulty correcting your correspondence, consider taking either a writing course at the local college or adult education program or a short business seminar on grammar and writing skills.

Chapter 5

Electronic Communication

$\mathcal{E}$lectronic communication has greatly increased our ability to keep in touch and the speed with which we can share information. However, with voice messages, fax, e-mail (electronic mail), pagers, and regular mail (dubbed "snail mail" due to it's relatively slow delivery in relation to e-mail), we often feel overburdened by the responsibility of responding to so much communication quickly.

The average businessperson sends and receives a total of about ninety messages a day. The same message may be sent several ways to make sure it gets through. Interruptions and the demand for an immediate reply are becoming overwhelming. E-mail, fax, phone, and postal mail messages pile up. The idea of saving time by using quick forms of communication has, in a sense, backfired. The timesaving speed of electronic communication has significantly added to our workload.

A public relations director lamented that while she was at lunch, she had twelve phone messages. It took over forty-five minutes to listen to the messages and even longer to respond to them. To listen, read, and respond to so much correspondence could take the entire day to the exclusion of any other work you need to do! Although business is conducted electronically at an incredible pace, the same rules of etiquette apply. E-mail and faxes should be written in memo or letter form. Keep in mind that you are communicating with busy people who do not wish to have intrusions, who may not have time for idle chitchat, but who may enjoy knowing that you were thinking of them and are working on their project.

Being on-line is being connected to other computers and users via communication lines: telephone lines, DSL (Digital Subscriber Line, a telephone line), cable, or wireless. On-line communication occurs when you work on an inter-office network or access the Internet or World Wide Web from your computer. All successful and growing businesses use computers in some way and generally have access to the Internet. E-mail, fax, and instant messages are important business tools that are becoming standard as people become more technologically literate. Business documents are frequently transmitted via e-mail or fax, including:

* Memos
* Meeting agendas
* Proposals and contracts
* Brochures
* News or research articles
* Newsletters
* Résumés

Many business relationships are no longer conducted in person. Communication is by fax, e-mail, and pager. Regardless of the communication form, there are guidelines of good business and courtesy that must be followed. Because the communication is not in person and because e-mail is fast, informal, and accomplished via electronics it lacks the common communication cues that come from voice inflection, facial expression, and body language. Your choice of words becomes an even more critical part of your communicating.

Electronic communication is fast. In many cases speed is essential to get the contract submitted and signed. Increasing use of electronic communications has significant impact on our business skills.

Consequently:

* You will need a strong vocabulary as words are often misinterpreted.
* Proper grammar is more important than ever. You must construct sentences correctly to accurately convey your meaning.
* You must develop the skills to express yourself clearly and concisely, both verbally and in writing.

NETIQUETTE

Netiquette, or net etiquette, comprises the courteous guidelines for communicating on-line via the Internet, also known as the World Wide Web. We need guidelines because more and more of us communicate using electronic means. University programs have been designed to address this newly emerging area of communication. With the use of e-mail comes a new language and a set of rules and responsibilities known as Netiquette.

E-MAIL ETIQUETTE

Although e-mail is a fast, convenient way to keep in touch with many people, it has a drawback: it is impersonal. E-mail users have developed ways to express emotion with capitals, abbreviations, and character combinations. For instance, the three punctuation symbols :-) are read as a happy face; LOL means laughing-out-loud; HEY or any word in all capital letters is the equivalent of shouting. E-mail has a language of its own, and you don't always know whether your receiver will understand it. By keeping your use of e-mail specific language to a minimum, you can avoid confusing your recipient. Use the same proper English, grammar, and spelling you would use in any business correspondence. Make e-mail messages simple and as brief as possible so the recipient can read them quickly and respond accordingly.

According to the Forrester Research Group (reported in the *Claris Guide of E-mail Etiquette*) "By the year 2005 users will be sending more than 5 billion personal messages a day." On-line communication is fast, efficient, and timesaving. Anyone with access to the necessary equipment can communicate by e-mail regardless of which service provider they use or where they are located.

Your e-mail should be concise and to the point and should reflect the same courtesy and common sense as your other business communications. Spontaneous thoughts or reminders are good subjects for e-mail. Avoid "flaming"—sending an angry or faultfinding e-mail message. Asterisks (*) are used in some e-mail systems to highlight a key word or for emphasis; don't overuse them. Some e-mail programs allow you to use boldface, italics, and even colors, but the recipient's e-mail program may not support such formatting. Letter forms used for standard forms of correspondence can be used for e-mail.

Allow the recipient an opportunity to receive and respond to your message. In these days of instant messages, we often expect an instant response.

Sending E-Mail Messages

❖ Provide a personal name in the top address.

❖ Always include a subject line in your message.

❖ Keep the message brief. Focus on one subject.

❖ Use correct spelling and grammar.

Replying to E-Mail Messages

❖ Include enough of the original e-mail message in your response to provide continuity. Avoid the temptation to add your response after each original e-mail statement. For example: Did Mary Smith from Myers Co. phone you last week? *Yes, she called Thursday.* I think we should plan a meeting with her to discuss the project. Let me know when you are available and I'll call her. *April 4 will work for me.* Have you reviewed the copy of the plans? *Yes.*

❖ Do not send an angry message.

❖ Be aware of where and to whom your reply is addressed. It may seem efficient to select an automatic "reply" or "answer" but your return message may not reach the sender. The return address attached to the original message may not be the sender's and your response may go to all the e-mail addresses the original message was sent to, not just to the sender.

Many firms use e-mail to advertise their business. Other unsolicited e-mail invites you to visit web sites of different types. Unsolicited e-mail or e-mail advertising is like junk mail and is annoying to most e-mail users. Unsolicited e-mail of this type, known as *spam*, is generally sent to thousands of e-mail addresses at once, a practice know as *spamming*. Service providers often offer methods to restrict the kinds of e-mail you receive. Many e-mail users also receive jokes and chain mail. Jokes can be fun to receive and to send to friends, but be aware that sending them to others may be perceived as frivolous and unprofessional, not to mention a waste of time. Don't e-mail jokes to business colleagues or clients; chain e-mail should not be forwarded.

Many warnings of viruses sent via e-mail are hoaxes and fall into the same category as chain e-mail. Some virus warnings are simply efforts to stop a particularly bothersome chain letter. If you are unsure about a virus warning, check the Computer Incident Advisory Capability (CIAC) Internet Website maintained by the U.S. Department of Energy: http://ciac.llnl.gov/ciac/CIACHoaxes.html. You can learn how to identify a new hoax or a valid warning.

It's easy to send duplicates of the same message by mistake, be careful what you send, particularly if you send the same e-mail to multiple recipients. Many e-mail providers offer shortcuts to e-mail one message to several addresses, often referred to as a *distribution list.* This is particularly useful if you wish to distribute an e-mail memo or other document to several people at once. You can minimize the appearance of a long distribution list by using a blind courtesy copy (BCC). Each recipient in the distribution list then sees only his name at the top of the message. E-mail software packages vary. Not all features are available with all providers. Check with your provider to learn more about the special features they offer for e-mail.

You can also develop your logo for your e-mail messages. You can write a "signature," which includes your name, title, e-mail address, postal mail address, phone, fax and other information you wish. Some people include a business slogan or a favorite quote. Your signature can be designed to be inserted at the end of all your e-mail messages or inserted by the push of a key. Your signature adds your personal touch to your electronic correspondence. Consider the length, number of words, spacing, and line length of your signature. Keep the signature lines close to your name and limit yourself to five lines because the receiver may not see the lines below your name. Again, check with your provider to learn if the signature feature is available to you.

The following is a sample signature. The closure would follow the text of the e-mail message with the name and address following:

Sandra Jones
1024 Skyview Lane
High Ridge, CA 90000-1111
707-555-1234 FAX 707-555-5678
I am a personal business coach who loves to help small
businesses.

For best results in using a specialized *signature* on your e-mail, keep your signature short, use your business slogan or choose a quote that is meaningful to you, and keep line length to sixty to seventy characters. Some e-mail programs do not accept lines of more than eighty characters.

The growing use of e-mail, which allows us to be connected with friends, family, clients, and colleagues, also enables us to reach the otherwise unreachable. You can locate almost anyone from an old college chum to the Queen of England. You can also locate hundreds of businesses and other resources. If you've ever wanted to write your senator, there will be an e-mail address you can use. In general, the address for our senators is: senator@senatorlastname.senate.gov; for example, to e-mail Senator Diane Wise, use the address: senator@wise.senate.gov.

E-mail has many advantages over regular mail. You can send your messages at any time of the day or night, on weekends or holidays, and recipients can read them at their leisure. E-mail does not use any of the receiver's office supplies, as standard fax does. Longer documents can be sent via e-mail rather than by fax, saving the recipient the expense of having to print many pages on special (thermal) fax paper.

Personal e-mail messages may be sent quickly between errands, while on the phone, or as quick hellos. Poorly prepared messages can cause misunderstandings, therefore poor grammar and misplaced informality must be avoided in business. Because e-mail is so fast, painless, and easy, one needs to be acutely sensitive to the possibility that the receiver has dozens of messages daily. Keeping your message short is the key, unless this is a personal friend with whom you have virtual chats rather than voice conversations. Those messages, of course, should not be written or read during business hours!

E-mail to or from a corporate address may be monitored, whether it is personal or business-related e-mail. Corporate monitoring of e-mail and Internet access is a controversial issue. Be aware that many companies believe it is in their best interest to monitor on-line use by their employees. Deletion of e-mail after it's read does not necessarily render it immune to such monitoring. Clandestine business deals, romances, and unauthorized divulgence of corporate secrets have been exposed by e-mail monitoring.

You will need to be on-line frequently to send, receive, and respond to e-mail in a timely manner. Many are not techno-literate; they are business professionals nonetheless and deserve respect. Be considerate and accommodate those who do not use e-mail; some of your business may depend upon it. Be sure all parties involved in any negotiation are kept informed, even if they are not on-line.

E-Mail Memos

Interoffice e-mail memos are common because most computers or terminals are connected via an office network. Many coworkers communicate by e-mail because they are always connected to the network. Sending e-mail to busy people is nonintrusive and considerate of the other person's time. They don't have to stop whatever they are doing to acknowledge or respond.

When you send an interoffice memo via e-mail, include all recipients' names, listed by corporate hierarchy. Keep all memos brief. Send memos only when necessary.

Many e-mail programs offer a "read receipt" feature that returns a notice or "receipt" when the e-mail message is displayed by the recipient. The receipt feature is useful when you are sending time-critical information or when you need confirmation your memo has been received. Message recipients may choose not to send a receipt even if one is requested. If your memo is especially time-critical or is expected, a brief phone call alerting the recipient may be necessary.

Instant Messaging

Instant Messaging (IM) is a feature that enables you to communicate instantly with another on-line user whenever you are both on-line. Some IM programs can alert you when users you select are on-line.

IM users may send instant messages directly to other on-line users, engage in one-on-one chat, and bypass the common delays and server problems in sending e-mail. An IM user may send an instant message rather than an e-mail message to alert friends, colleagues, or important professional sources their communiquÈ has been received. There will be times when a short phone call may be more time effective than an instant message chat simply because the IM must be typed and not all users are speedy typists!

Instant messaging is part e-mail and part on-line chat. An instant message is received immediately, whereas e-mail may take thirty seconds, a few minutes, an hour, or possibly even longer before it is received.

Not all business professionals are receptive to interruptions while they are working on-line, the prime time for instant messaging. Instant messages may interrupt other important on-line work. Exercise thoughtful judgement in using instant messages. Your colleague several doors down may welcome the occasional instant message, but your client across town may find your instant message intrusive. Some IM software includes options to block incoming messages.

Features of IM software vary. In addition to blocking unwanted IM or alerting when other users are on-line, IM software can also be used for multiple-party conferences in private chat rooms. Check with your service provider for more detailed information.

Some IM and chat programs require all participants have the same software. Many of these may be downloaded free of charge from the internet or are available from your service provider. Be cautious as downloading programs to your computer can introduce unwanted computer viruses.

The Special Language of E-Mail

E-mail language symbols, known as *emoticons,* are appearing even in some business e-mail. There are too many emoticons (like the smiley face, :-)) and related symbols to list here. Be aware that they exist and use them sparingly, if at all, in your business communications. They are not always generally known or accepted as proper etiquette.

Acronyms are made up of the first letter of words, capitalized and put together to shorten a frequently used phrase, such as FYI for For

Your Information. Many other acronyms commonly used in e-mail or chat rooms are less well known and not necessarily proper in terms of etiquette. Don't mystify your client with an acronym like TTFN, Ta Ta for Now.

INTERNATIONAL E-MAIL

International communications via e-mail save the expense of international phone calls (both fax and voice) and overnight mail delivery, the long waiting for correspondence to cross the world, and the need to make and accept phone calls at inconvenient hours. E-mail cuts across the world's cultures and spans the time zones. However, it does not eliminate cultural nuances that must be respected.

International e-mail requires some additional considerations. E-mails may arrive during off hours, on holidays, or during vacations. It should not come as a surprise that other countries observe different holidays and customs than we do in the United States. Some international businesses close for a month during the summer or winter solstice. Just because e-mail is fast and inexpensive, it doesn't guarantee a speedy reply or even a reply at all whether in the United States or abroad. Technology is not nearly as advanced in other parts of the world as it is in the United States. I have friends in Europe whose e-mail server shuts down whenever it rains!

❖ Do not re-send an e-mail message until you have allowed ample time for it to be received and reviewed.

❖ Remember that weather or other circumstances may render phone lines inoperable from time to time.

❖ Remember also that the equipment to receive e-mail may not be as accessible as it is at your home or office, and this may contribute to a delay in response.

❖ Include date and time appropriate to your country when you send your e-mail.

❖ Include contact information with your complete international telephone area codes, address, and postal zip code in your signature. Include your country as a part the address.

❖ Be cautious of using humor or sarcasm. They do not translate well.

❖ Note that currency figures should be indicated by country or the financial terminology used for financial transactions. U.S. dollars are generally used to monitor the exchange rate. Indicate U.S. for U.S. currency, yen for Japanese money, pesetas for Spanish money, pound (£) for English money, etc. Be accurate where you place your decimal point and commas in currency amounts.

FAX ETIQUETTE

Proper etiquette requires that you send a cover page when you send a fax. The cover sheet should include the recipient's name, sender's name, date, and the number of pages being transmitted. A brief statement describing the purpose of the fax may also be included on the cover page. Use a standard, easily readable font set in a 12- to 16-point size. The larger type size calls attention to your fax and is easily readable. Just don't let it get too big! I personally prefer the recipient's name and other information in 16 point and the text in 14 point. If you prefer, you can use bold to emphasize the recipient's name.

The cover sheet should include a line describing the subject of the fax. The receiver's name should appear clearly and boldly on the cover sheet. In rare instances, a cover sheet is not necessary. If you are speaking with the recipient immediately before you fax, ask if they need a cover sheet. As a fax recipient, if you don't need a cover sheet, ask the sender to omit it. Omitting the cover sheet can save paper and the time to print it. However, proper fax etiquette requires the cover sheet; if you are not certain, include one. Also, as a courtesy, never send more than five pages without notifying the recipient prior to sending.

Materials you send by fax should have ample margins, as much as one- to 1½-inch margins all around. Fax machines are notorious for cutting off information that extends too close to the edges of the page. Some faxes actually reduce the document by 5 percent or more to avoid this problem. If the fax is urgent, call to confirm receipt of the fax and verify that it was received by the intended person. Use this opportunity to ask if there are any questions about the information sent and to confirm that all the pages were received.

As with e-mail, many businesses use faxes to advertise their products and services. Since the receiving business bears the cost of printing the fax, usually on expensive thermal paper, many businesses consider the advertisements to be expensive junk mail, also known as junk fax. Unsolicited faxes are not appreciated; don't send them. In fact, in some states it is illegal to send unsolicited faxes!

Electronic Signatures

Digital Signatures, also known as Electronic Signatures, are becoming more widely used in business and in internet commerce and transactions. On June 30, 2000, President Clinton signed The Electronic Signatures in Global and National Commerce Act. The E-SIGN Act gives an online "John Hancock" the same legal validity as a signature in pen and ink. Some of the legal reforms that will be needed to advance electronic signature technology and its acceptance fall under the jurisdiction of individual states, and many issues are yet to be resolved.

Presently, there are a number of internet companies offering verification and signature services to positively identify senders, recipients, and sources of information by digitally encoding and thereby both protecting and restricting access to electronically transmitted material. Questions as to whether an electronic signature is legally binding remain. Often, a duplicate of the electronic document is printed and signed by pen and ink to satisfy the need for a legally recognized document.

Chapter 6

When You Speak

*M*ore than 75 percent of new contacts make their decision about whether or not to do further business with you during the initial phone call. Make that initial phone contact and all the succeeding ones, the very best possible. We use office phones, cell phones, conference calls, and speaker phones to get business completed. The person you talk with on the phone cannot see the size of your office, your office furnishings, or you. All their conclusions about you, your business, and your ability to deliver what you promise, are based on your voice and your words and how well they convey courtesy and respect. What kind of an impression do you leave when you speak on the telephone?

Your voice is your vehicle for communication. Record a phone call or tape-record yourself speaking and listen to your voice. You want to speak loudly and clearly enough for people to hear you easily. If people ask you to repeat things you say, you may not be speaking loudly enough. Make certain that your voice is pleasant and causes people to want to listen. Practice your speaking to develop variety in pace, modulation, and pitch. The way you speak impacts the way you are perceived. Is your voice pitch high (shrill) or very low (deep)? Listen to your voice with an unbiased friend who will help you evaluate the quality and listening appeal of your voice. The most comfortable listening range falls within the medium range. High-pitched voices are more difficult to understand and are often perceived as unprofessional. Speech, voice, or drama coaches can help you improve your voice. You'll hear results right away, and they'll make a positive impact on your professionalism.

Your voice and words are essential to making a positive impression and portraying your professionalism. Using proper telephone manners will help you build friends and clients, develop and keep a good reputation, and lead to success.

TELEPHONE ETIQUETTE

Whenever you speak on the telephone, speak clearly and directly into the mouthpiece. Identify yourself immediately to the other person. Speak slowly and with courtesy. Focus yourself on the purpose of the call and the person you are speaking with; don't try to do things like open mail or talk with someone in the room with you in the course of your telephone conversation. Don't eat or drink while you are on the phone. You may not be aware of how well the person at the other end of the line can hear you chewing and swallowing; the impression you leave will not be a good one. Smile as you speak. You'll be surprised how well a smile can be heard in your voice.

Making Phone Calls

- ❖ Be prepared before you dial. If this is an information gathering call, have a script handy so that you will remember to cover all the information.
- ❖ Know the reason for your call and be ready to discuss it.
- ❖ Place your call during normal business hours. Your call will not be well received if you wait until five minutes before closing.
- ❖ Be ready to leave a message with an assistant or receptionist if the person you wish to talk with is unavailable.
- ❖ Make your own calls. Asking your assistant to get a client on the phone implies to the client that your time is more valuable than theirs.
- ❖ Answer phone messages left for you within forty-eight hours, whenever possible. If you are away for more than a day, it is courteous to your callers to so indicate in your message unless someone is taking your calls for you.

Answering Phone Calls

If you are the administrative assistant or receptionist who handles incoming calls for your company, you are the voice of the company. You are the first contact a person has with your business whether you are a one-person office or a large corporation. This is true for anyone who answers incoming calls, regardless of their position. You can make a good impression when speaking on the phone when you

- ❖ Answer by the third or fourth ring.
- ❖ Identify yourself immediately.
- ❖ Speak slowly, clearly, and with courtesy.
- ❖ Speak with a smile in your voice.
- ❖ Use the caller's name.
- ❖ Have pen and paper handy to make notes or take a message.
- ❖ Minimize background noise.
- ❖ End the call with a positive statement and an acknowledgment of the caller.

"Please Hold"

There will be times when you will need to put callers on hold. Only put callers on hold for a few seconds. If the call is being transferred, make sure the other party picks up the phone in a reasonable amount of time. If they do not, pick up the call again, acknowledge the caller by name, and ask if they would like to continue to hold or if they would rather leave a message.

If you must leave the line to answer a call-waiting call, make sure you leave the first caller on hold for only a few seconds, and acknowledge the caller by name when you return. Remember that call-waiting is a convenience for you, not your caller. When you ask the first caller to wait while you answer a second call, you imply that he is less important than the new caller. Make your connection with the second caller brief; return their call promptly when you finish with the first caller.

If you need to transfer a call, explain the reason for the transfer to the caller. Monitor the lines to be certain the transfer was completed successfully.

Sometimes, you may be required to answer someone else's phone while they are away from their desk or to answer the phone for others in your office. This can be challenging when you must answer questions or provide information that you do not have. The best response is to take a message. Be sure that there are phone message pads and pen where you will answer the phone. Ask for the caller's name, phone number (repeat it for accuracy), reason for the call, and best time to return the call. Add your name or initials and the date and time of the call to the message.

A courteous response to the caller is that the person they wish to reach is unavailable. You may add that they are with a client, in a meeting, or have stepped away from their desk for a moment. Be aware that you want to leave a professional image with the caller. It is not important for the caller to know exactly where the person is, what they are doing at the moment, or even where you think they might be. In fact, to offer this level of information may betray confidentiality and imply that you are not careful about preserving confidentiality for your colleagues or your clients.

Handling Difficult Callers

Sometimes callers are rude and unreasonable. You may not know why they are rude or unhappy, but you can influence the outcome of the call and perhaps regain the caller's goodwill. Begin by remaining calm and speaking in even tones. Ask the caller to identify himself and ask the reason for the call. Speaking softly will encourage the caller to calm down and not shout. If the caller uses obscenities, ask them to use other language. Explain that you can't help them if they won't help you. When speaking with the caller, address him as *Mr.* Jones and *sir* (use *ma'am* with a woman caller).

Angry people are not ready to listen. They must get their anger out before they will be able to listen to you. Encourage them to explain the problem or why they are unhappy. Restate the problem to them, and offer to transfer them to the appropriate department or suggest someone with whom they should speak. Offer to see if that person is available and, if not, offer to take a message. You may be able to diffuse some of the caller's anger just by listening attentively. This will make your colleague's job easier when he has to talk with this caller and will leave the caller with a more positive impression of your company.

VOICE MESSAGING SYSTEMS

Voice messaging systems were developed to provide more efficient customer service and to improve the productivity of office staff. Unfortunately, many customers wait a long time through layers and layers of messages making numerical choices based on questions asked to them. They often never get to a real person and either are asked to leave a message or have to hang up and start the process over again.

Voice messaging systems serve a purpose but they can be frustrating to callers. Frequently callers have difficulty knowing which selections to make to have their question answered. They are left feeling frustrated; the company has lost their personal touch and perhaps a customer. We've probably all had experiences with a voice messaging system. Maybe you've come across a message like the following.

> *Hello, you have reached ACE Company. To order a product—press 1, to ask about a charge on your bill—press 2, to review your bill—press 4, to speak to the operator—press 0. Hello, you have reached the automated system for ACE. If you wish to speak to someone about a warranty—press 1, if you wish to speak to a customer service representative—press 3, if you wish to speak to the operator—press 4. Hello, you have reached the automated system for ACE. To report a lost or stolen card—press 1, to increase your credit limit—press 2, to speak to an operator—press 3. . . . pause . . . Hello, all our operators are busy helping other customers. Your call is important to us so please stay on the line . . . music . . . we estimate the next available service representative will be with you in five minutes.*

When someone finally answers, you may have reached a department in error and have to start the system over again, or the person you've reached may not know how to transfer you to the correct department and you may get cut off (and have to start over again).

Some voice messaging systems allow callers to bypass the message by pressing a specified telephone button such as the pound (#) key. If your message system has a long message and you have frequent callers, tell them how to bypass the remainder of the message early in the message.

Call your own company or business and put yourself in the shoes of your client or customer. I know a company president who was traveling on business. He phoned the company to speak with one of his sales managers but couldn't get through. In desperation, he called the customer service line and got locked into the voice message loop. He was shocked by how inefficient and frustrating the system was. Does your company answering machine message or voice message system leave a positive impression? You may wish to periodically check your own message system to be sure.

YOUR TELEPHONE GREETING

When leaving a telephone greeting on your answering machine or voice mail system that will be heard by your callers speak slowly and state your name, company, and/or phone number. Keep the message brief; some systems will only allow thirty to sixty seconds for your greeting. Ask the caller for specific information, for example, "Please leave your name and phone number."

If you have unlimited time for your greeting, you can make the message interesting and fun. You can play music in the background, leave a favorite quote, or make a comment about business or life. Whatever you choose, consider its impact on the positive impression you want your message to make on your clients.

If the caller can bypass the message, give instructions on how to do so in the message. If you can be reached by pager or other means, include instructions to that effect also.

LEAVING A MESSAGE

When leaving a message for someone you have called speak slowly and clearly. Leave your name, phone number, and a brief message. Say your phone number slowly; many people repeat the number so quickly that the recipient can't write it down or hear the numbers. If you say the number too fast, you may not get the return phone call. Give your phone number twice when leaving a message, once at the beginning of the message and again at the end. Mention the best time to return your call.

If you don't really need a return call, it is considerate to leave enough information about why you are calling to enable the person you've called to take care of the matter. For instance, if you're calling to confirm your lunch appointment, remind the individual of the date, time, and place. Let them know they don't need to call you back unless there is a problem or they need to reschedule. It is always proper etiquette to leave your phone number even if you know they have it; your thoughtfulness will save them the time and effort of looking up your number.

At the end of the message leave your name and phone number again, as a courtesy to the recipient so they don't have to rewind the tape if they didn't hear your name or phone number clearly the first time.

CELL PHONE ETIQUETTE

Is the person with whom you are eating lunch, having a meeting, attending a conference, church, concert, or other event less important than someone who might call you on your cell phone? When you answer your cell phone without considering those around you, you send them the message that they aren't as important. Having a cell phone is not a status symbol; in fact it may be a rudeness badge. Cell phones are a modern technology convenience to allow us to keep on top of every business deal and to be quickly accessible to anyone who might have a question or need assistance. But there is a price to pay for that instant availability.

When your cell phone is on, you are at the beck and call of all who have your number. You will feel a need to answer and act on calls as if they are more urgent than your current activity. You risk being interrupted and distracted at inappropriate and inconvenient times. It is not necessary for everyone to have your cell phone number; be thoughtful about who you want to be able to reach you by cell phone.

Cell phones are most effective when used to call for help, to collect messages, and to make urgent calls while away from the office. If you are driving alone in slow traffic, a call may make efficient use of your time.

Cell phone use is inconsiderate of those around you when you use it in enclosed public places such as restaurants, elevators, subways, airplanes, buses, and trains. Your call may be annoying to others in churches, synagogues, concerts, theaters, waiting rooms, courtrooms (you could be fined or asked to leave), or other quiet public places.

And remember, when you use your cell phone, make sure you don't say anything you wouldn't want to be repeated or stated on a billboard.

I was disturbed by a man who paced the dentist's waiting room and conducted a business call while I sat within earshot of every word. I was annoyed, as was the office staff. Such behavior is rude and inconsiderate. I imagine the person on the other end of the phone would not have been pleased if they'd realized their call was so public. It would have been better for the man to step outside or sit in his car for the time it took to transact the call.

Should I turn off my cell phone at the dining table?
Yes. If you must accept a call, alert your host or guests when you sit down. When the phone rings, excuse yourself from the table and keep your conversation private and brief. Whenever you are dining in a restaurant, even if dining alone, leave the room if you must talk on the cell phone to avoid disturbing other diners.

At a luncheon program, the woman across the table took out her cell phone, dialed, and then covering her mouth to muffle her voice, proceeded to conduct "quiet" business. Her actions were rude to the luncheon speaker (who was in the midst of his speech), to those at her table and, in fact, to all in seeing and hearing distance. If you need to be working or checking important messages, leave the table and move to a private place where you won't disturb others. Do not assume that just because you turn your back to the crowd or cover your mouth while you talk on the phone that you are practicing acceptable etiquette. Talking on your cell phone, allowing the ring to be heard or a pager to beep, is rude and annoying to the others around you no matter where you are.

Cell phone use while driving increases the risk of auto accidents by more than 30 percent. Consider using an ear phone accessory with your cell phone to keep your hands free while driving. Pull your car over to the side of the road or onto a side street if you receive a business call. You will be better able to focus on the individual calling and the business under discussion. Your caller will appreciate the implication that his call is important to you. Otherwise, you are creating a dangerous situation for other drivers and their passengers. Always ask yourself, "Do I need to make or take this call at this moment?" Beware of jeopardizing the safety of others.

If you use a cell phone:

❖ Don't force others who happen to be wherever you are to listen to your cell phone calls.

❖ Don't call your cell phone friends from outside of their area code if you can avoid it, especially since they will be paying for the long-distance charges.

❖ Don't drive under the influence of an absorbing conversation.

❖ Don't ask to use a friend's cell phone.

❖ Don't call friends who reserve their cell phone only for emergencies.

Observe the rules of common sense and good etiquette when using cell phones. A simple way to remind yourself of the on or off status of your phone is to wear it on your waist when it is on and you are accepting calls, and put it in your briefcase or bag when you don't wish to receive calls and your phone is off. Call a cell phone only if the individual has instructed you to call or if you have determined that an immediate answer is imperative.

If you need the convenience of a cell phone when traveling abroad you can rent a global cell phone through your local wireless carrier. By making the arrangements with my carrier, I can continue to use my U.S. cell phone number as I travel.

VIDEOCONFERENCING

Videoconferencing is increasingly common even though it involves a considerable initial investment. It requires that all the individuals have a video camera and compatible software on their computer. The computer needs a camera installed above the monitor as well as software and hardware compatible with that of others participating in the videoconference. We see more videoconferencing as a mode of communication because it helps to avoid the long, frequent, and/or expensive flights to attend important meetings. Videoconferences minimize travel costs, reduce wear and tear on the travelers, and save time. Critical documents can be sent in advance by fax to increase the effectiveness of the videoconference.

Videoconferencing is practical but comes with challenges. Some rules of etiquette need to be closely followed or disaster can result. Interrupting a speaker is one of the biggest problems. It takes some practice to know when to interject your own comments during a conference with others. Greater emphasis is placed on facial expressions, voice, word choice, gestures, and body language because the element of personal contact is missing. Your gestures and habits are magnified by video. Precise, concise communication is important. There is little allowance for looking around, nose rubbing, ear pulling, or grooming. Videoconferencing is not like telephone communication; your every movement is in view. Your appearance is critical for professional credibility and for making an effective presentation.

Videoconferencing is used by medical specialists to consult on critical patients or operations, for depositions and other legal purposes, for meetings of a company's board of directors, and for a variety of other meetings and consultations.

The same rules of etiquette apply to videoconferencing that apply to other business meetings and appointments. Electronic setup and advance preparation time is required. Confirm the appointment well in advance, have equipment on and tested, and be ready and smiling at the appointment time. Keep to the agenda, which has been sent to the other parties prior to the meeting. Keep track of time with a nearby clock. This is your opportunity to make your professional impression with style and confidence. Look at the camera, avoid offensive gestures or habits like gum chewing or yawning, and keep your hands away from your face. Sit straight in your chair to project a competent professional.

TELECONFERENCING

Teleconferencing by phone is a practical way to conduct a meeting. All participants should follow the guidelines set by the chair. The chair calls the meeting and maintains full control of the meeting to avoid digression. The chair should call the roll by having everyone introduce themselves with their self-introduction, (see *Introducing Yourself,* Chapter 1, The First Impression) including any specifics asked for by the leader. The rules for speaking need to be outlined and reiterated if someone does not follow them.

Voice-only communication forces attention to your voice inflection and word choice. The basic rules for teleconferencing are the same as those for any business communication: don't interrupt, keep on the subject, and avoid negative comment of others. Without body language, which is a major part of your communication, you must rely primarily on your words and voice to communicate your ideas. Enunciate clearly and smile often. You project positive inflections in your voice when you smile.

Everyone must call in on time, as prearranged. The leader must be specific about the time and the time zone so that everyone knows when the meeting is scheduled to begin. An agenda should be distributed before the call and reiterated at the beginning of the conference call itself.

The cost per participant will vary depending on the long-distance provider so beware if you are "on the road" and calling in for period of time. You may wish to use an 800 number if one is available for this purpose. Some organizations call each of the participants from the central meeting point and thus absorb the telephone costs for the participants.

When participants speak, they should preface their remarks by stating their name. Participants may be assigned speaking turns, or the session may be an open discussion. It is essential that there be no "out of turn" interruptions. If you wish to speak, wait for a pause to begin your contribution. Keep the discussion to the business or agenda of the meeting.

At the end of the conference the leader should summarize the discussion, close the conference, and thank the participants. A written outline should be e-mailed or faxed to participants within three days of the call. Teleconferencing can be very useful to gather people from many different locations together. The leader must maintain control of the discussion to keep it on the topic and moving forward.

THE ART OF CONVERSATION

Making conversation is a skill that can be improved. The art of making conversation is cultivated. Choose your topics carefully when conducting business. Avoid topics of religion, politics, diet, personal philosophy, spouses, ethnic jokes, and health. Conversing is easier for some people than for others, but practice and thought help to master the art. Asking questions and giving compliments are part of good conversation. People like to talk about themselves and their activities, so learn to be a good listener.

When making compliments, be sincere. You needn't respond to a compliment with a compliment. Be cautious about giving compliments to everyone all of the time. Compliments that make mention of body parts, necklines, clothing fit, and how someone walks or moves, could be grounds for harassment regardless of your intentions.

Accepting a compliment can seem awkward. When someone pays you a compliment, your response need only be, "Thank you, I appreciate your noticing," or just "Thank you." Often we feel a little embarrassed and think that we have to make some qualifying response. When someone compliments your tie or dress and you respond, "Oh, this old thing!" you are, in a sense, rejecting their compliment. Instead, just smile and say "Thank you."

Keep in mind that you are creating and maintaining a relationship. Be friendly and use common sense while being courteous and respectful. Learn to talk about subjects other than your work. You want to be perceived as well-rounded and informed on a variety of subjects, not just by the people you meet, but also by your employer. Your career advancement may hinge on your ability to discuss subjects other than your work.

Naturally, there will be times when it is appropriate for you to talk about work. When you talk about work, be aware of the others with whom you are speaking. Every industry has its own language and not everyone will be familiar with yours. You'll have a better conversation and communicate your ideas more clearly if you avoid jargon and industry-specific terms. After all, the goal of all communication is to enhance understanding, not to confuse. Your listeners will appreciate your efforts.

Conversation Topics

Should I talk about my kids? Should I mention my new car?
What do I say? What should I avoid?
Get ready, get set for conversation! Here are some suggestions for conversation topics.

Ask the other person questions about vacations, movies they've seen recently, any books they may have read recently, whether they follow any of the local sports teams, or even if they see any trends in the business market. Pursue subjects they are interested in.

Some subjects of conversation are best avoided. These include

- ❖ Religious topics
- ❖ Politics
- ❖ Diet and weight
- ❖ Talking about your spouse, except in general terms
- ❖ Talking about coworkers
- ❖ Gossip
- ❖ Criticism
- ❖ Swear words
- ❖ Jokes with ethnic undertones
- ❖ Lengthy personal stories

To prepare yourself for conversation, try reading the daily paper, trade journals, or weekly magazines. When reading the newspaper, look for interesting articles in the following sections:

❖ Sports pages

❖ Lifestyle sections

❖ Business section

❖ Travel section

❖ Book and movie reviews

There are many sources for conversation topics. Be creative, follow your own interests and try new things. Radio and TV news programs are good sources for current events and what others think of them. Lectures and conferences are held on a variety of subjects and may spark a new interest or suggest a new perspective on a familiar subject. It's always fun to attend plays, concerts, and sporting events, and these are all interesting to talk about with others. Perhaps you are involved in your community and would enjoy sharing information about community activities.

You certainly don't need to be an expert in all topics. Read the headlines and skim through a paragraph or two of the articles that interest you. Having some comments on a few current subjects can serve as an excellent way to get a conversation going.

As you converse with others, listen, laugh, and smile often. Be aware of how your body language and gestures encourage those you are speaking with to relax and to participate. Don't take yourself so seriously that you can't laugh at yourself. We all have stories to tell, many humorous. If appropriate, share one of yours!

The only way that you can meet and talk with interesting people is to be one yourself. Cultivate your own interests, pick and choose the articles, programs, and places that interest you. Continue to learn new things; that is what makes you an interesting person.

My 87-year-old mother is interesting to talk with. She watches sports and knows who has won or lost. She reads the paper and can talk about a variety of TV programs. She also watches game shows for trivia information.

Naturally, there will be times when you need to leave or close a conversation during a party or social function. There are many ways you may close a conversation gracefully by following some etiquette guidelines. You may excuse yourself with the explanation that you would like to go to some other area or activity at the function, perhaps the buffet table or exhibit table; make sure you actually go there, not to another conversation. Tell the person you've enjoyed talking with them and suggest you both move on to meet others. Another method is to thank them for their interest in your business and wish them well in their own.

If you are talking with a small group and you notice another person who might like to join your conversation, step back to open the circle of the conversation. By turning your body slightly toward the newcomer you use your body language to invite him to join the conversation. Once this person begins to join in the conversation, you may excuse yourself from the group. Proper etiquette requires that you not leave a newcomer alone and move on to speak to others until you draw a new person into the current conversation.

Magic Words

Most of us learned about "magic words" when we were growing up. The magic in the words comes from how they are used to express respect and courtesy towards others. Using the magic words evokes a response that affects attitude, body language, and emotion in the person to whom you are speaking. Use them everyday. They will smooth the path of your career and improve your relationships with others, both business and social.

Please	Thank you
You're welcome	Excuse me
I'm sorry	Hello
Good morning	Good night
Good-bye	
How are you?	
(Be sure you listen for the response!)	

It is simple to weave these words into your everyday conversation. When you use these words regularly you will quickly note how much more willing people are to listen, respond, and agree to your requests. We bristle and resist when we are pushed verbally or physically. Using the magic words makes a difference in your communication and in the responses you receive to your ideas and requests.

PUBLIC SPEAKING

Public speaking and making conversation are two essential skills in the business world. Being an interesting person to others takes effort on your part. Your colleagues and clients will more likely want to spend time with you and to seek your advice when you have evidenced a broad knowledge and interest in a variety of subjects. No one expects you to be an expert in everything. Develop a hobby, attend local musical performances, read a few books, and travel. Learn the history of your area. Knowledge does not suddenly descend upon you; it is a lifetime pursuit.

Many people can only talk about business or their work. Their life is so focused on their career that it negatively impacts their ability to make new friends or contacts. Being too narrow in your conversation topics can impede your chance for promotion or for a new position in a different department. You should be skilled at speaking about your business, but not to the exclusion of all other topics.

In the course of a business career, almost everyone will have the opportunity or assignment to speak in public. You may be asked to make a presentation in the boardroom or at a sales meeting. Your boss may ask you to speak at an annual meeting, make a toast at a party, or present a project to a group of colleagues. If the thought of speaking in front of people strikes fear in your heart, you're not alone. Speaking in public is the number one fear most people share. If you are in business, and you want to be a success, you can expect to be called upon to speak at some time.

Here are some suggestions to help you prepare before you panic. Accept the fact that it will happen; you are going to speak in public. Next, develop your basic skills. It is important to know how to prepare a talk, write a presentation, time it (to fit time limitations), speak well, avoid distracting phrases and gestures, and be comfortable speaking before an audience. A number of organizations can help you, or you may take a class. Join a Toastmasters International group in your area. Most groups meet weekly for the specific purpose of practicing speaking before a group. Different Toastmasters Groups meet at different times of the day. They are generally a small and supportive group and offer you the opportunity to practice and learn basic skills. Your local chamber of commerce should be able to direct you to the groups in your area, or call Toastmasters International at 949-858-8255 (California).

More help is available from speech coaches, drama coaches, speechwriters, college courses on public speaking, and personal business coaches. You may also call the National Speakers Association (NSA) headquarters in Tempe, AZ, at 602-968-2552. They can direct you to someone in your area who can be of assistance. You can also look on the Internet for http://www.nsaspeaker.org or http://www.toastmasters.org to get started. There are many NSA members around the country who will gladly give you some pointers on how to improve your speaking skills.

Once you master the skills to speak well in front of others, you'll avoid heart palpitations and knee shaking. You'll be able to present your thoughts concisely and to feel comfortable, competent, and credible. You are not expected to be a fabulous speaker, but you will be respected for getting your point across clearly and with validity. It is not such a difficult task when you set your mind to it. Begin now to develop and polish your skills as a speaker; you will use them frequently in your career.

Verbal Style

Polishing your speaking skills requires consideration of your verbal style and voice. Each of us has a speaking style that we develop and modify over time. Your style reflects your inner being and is shaped by your experiences and education. You can modify your style to suit new situations and goals. You change your verbal communication by selecting precise words, using complete sentences, speaking without slang and dialect, and using the appropriate language for the industry and location.

Good enunciation and careful choice of words should be high on your improvement list. Your credibility and ultimately your level of promotion within the company will be affected by your speech. Pronounce words clearly and correctly. Avoid slurring syllables and dropping sounds from the ends of your words. Speaking too softly, using slang, and mumbling leave negative impressions. You and your immediate colleagues may all speak the same way, but if you have aspirations for a position in management or a position in another location, the way you sound when you speak and your verbal style will be important in achieving your goal.

Chapter 7

Preparing for the Job

*M*ost individuals will work at a minimum of three jobs in the course of their work lives. Many will change careers altogether. Few people spend their entire career working for a single employer anymore. Employees move from company to company for career advancement, money, travel opportunities, a more pleasant work environment, location, and other benefits.

To move ahead in your career, and sometimes just to keep up with the competition, you need to know how to prepare for an interview and interview well. You also need to keep your résumé current. Naturally, your work skills will also play a vital factor in advancing your career.

ETHICS

Your personal values, and the ways in which you act according to those values, are your ethics. The standards of conduct and moral judgement you believe in and demonstrate in your actions are an integral part of getting a job and keeping it, and of living a quality life. Your ethics apply to your business and how you work and are on display in everything you do and in every choice you make.

Your reputation for exercising ethical judgement will follow you. A person will judge your business values and standards by how they perceive your ethics. Be mindful that what you say and do should be perceived by others as ethical. Your accountability, your credibility, and your truthfulness all should reflect positively on you and the way you choose to conduct business.

You should consider carefully the ways in which you are perceived by others and their judgement of your abilities. Your association with others and how you conduct yourself in business and business-related situations are observed and become part of how other people evaluate your competence and credibility. Your loyalty, honesty, commitment, values, decency, and sense of right and wrong comprise your personal ethics.

The following are some of the ways that you can demonstrate good ethics in the workplace:

- Do not participate in gossip.
- Be courteous and respectful to superiors and to subordinates.
- Be positive and pleasant.
- Accept constructive criticism.
- Maintain personal dignity.
- Make an effort to preserve the dignity of another.
- Keep confidences and maintain confidentiality.
- Show your concern for others.
- Give credit to those deserving.
- Be honest.
- Keep your word.
- Encourage and help others to do their best.
- Make practical and constructive suggestions for improvement.

YOUR RÉSUMÉ (CURRICULUM VITAE)

In today's job market a curriculum vitae (CV, c.v., or vitae) should be part of your personal portfolio. A curriculum vitae contains your personal history and professional qualifications. It is comprised of your résumé, reference letter(s), and personal information pertinent to the job you are interested in. International firms use the term *curriculum vitae* rather than résumé.

Because workers today change jobs frequently, you need to have a current résumé prepared at all times. Your résumé may be the most important presentation you will make in the job search; make sure it is well prepared. Like a tailored suit, a résumé needs to be slightly altered as your experiences and history change. An effective résumé is a powerful tool. It should emphasize your skills and be presented in a clean, easy-to-read format that evidences your professionalism.

Résumé formats can be functional or chronological. The most common is the chronological, arranging work experience by years with the present job listed foremost. Job seekers in the traditional fields of business management and consulting find this format works best.

Those who are returning to the workplace after a period of not working or working in a nonrelated field, may find the functional résumé format more useful. This format focuses on types of jobs and skills, usually grouping them under such headings as "employee relations," "management," or "sales." The functional format is particularly effective for individuals seeking a career change and needing to highlight the qualities they bring to a new job.

To match your skills with what you believe the potential employer is looking for, create a statement of your "objective." One or two well-stated sentences matching your skills with what the employer is seeking helps your résumé stand out.

The primary goal of a résumé is to get an interview. Your résumé will need to catch the employer's attention.

- ❖ Use a concise format that is easy to read.
- ❖ Emphasize your experience and highlight your skills and qualifications.
- ❖ Avoid personal details about marital status, hobbies, and vacations unless they are specifically related to the job. These may be shared in the interview if appropriate.
- ❖ Show how you have used your skills and the results.
- ❖ Hand address the envelope.
- ❖ Use high-quality paper, in white, off-white, or a soft color.
- ❖ Avoid gimmicks. Don't send flowers or candy to get attention.

Many job seekers now consult with services that specialize in developing professional résumés. If you are unsure of how to proceed with writing your résumé, you may want to consider a résumé service, or you may consult your local library for references and how-to books. The recruiter is going to look at what your résumé says and how well the information is presented. Check the document for clean and attractive format, correct spelling, and accurate information.

Increasingly, résumés are being faxed or e-mailed to potential employers or posted with on-line services. Many résumés are scanned (copied) and retained in the computer system, filed by keywords. Employers that require résumés be submitted electronically or that plan to scan the résumé may require special formatting of the document.

INTERVIEWS

Either before or after submitting your application and résumé, gather information about the company. You may ask the company for any marketing literature or business reports they may have available for the public. An annual report can be useful to learn more about the company's financial position and also about the company's current plans and goals. Visit the library and check the Internet to gather information (many companies now have their own Websites). The more you learn about the company, the more interested and informed you will appear. At the same time, having that information will help you to determine whether you want to work for this company.

Many employers now conduct preliminary interviews over the phone. Often these calls are made at unexpected times and can be after work hours. You are expected to speak intelligently, just as if you were sitting down together in a formal interview setting. You will be evaluated on your spontaneity and ability to communicate. The call may seem like just a casual phone conversation, but it is, in fact, an interview. Someone may call you to chat, ask if you are still interested in the job, and then tell you that someone will be calling to set up an interview.

There may be several phone conversations before you actually have a formal interview. The phone screening process saves hiring personnel time by prequalifying potential employees.

The personal interview normally takes place at the business offices. After the interview and before hiring, you may be invited to spend a day at the facility. There, your interview may be continued as you meet with representatives from different departments, particularly when you are given a tour of the facility where you will meet with several management staff. A meal with various members of the company may be included. Sometimes the meal is a casual cafeteria-style meeting, while other times you will be taken off site or invited to dinner after office hours. However the company conducts the interview, you are always being observed to determine if you fit the corporate image and can work with the team.

After an interview how long should I wait to before I call and ask if I am hired?

During the course of the interview ask about the hiring process and when the final hiring decision will be made. Ask if you can call and speak with a specific person. Call on the specified day. Ask if the decision has been made; request information about future available positions, if you are not hired. Always write a thank you note immediately after the interview.

When you attend the interview, dress appropriately; wear the clothes you would wear for the job or the next job up. It's a good idea to arrive about fifteen minutes before the interview. Be prepared for the interview; know current details about the company. Use proper etiquette during the interview; you want to leave a positive impression.

- ❖ Use the rest room to check buttons, zippers, teeth, face, hair, hands, and clothing for best appearance.
- ❖ Get rid of chewing gum, toothpicks, etc.
- ❖ Speak with confidence.
- ❖ Stand to shake hands with all the persons in the room.
- ❖ Sit straight in the chair.
- ❖ Use eye contact and smile frequently.
- ❖ Do not enter the interview with the smell of (tobacco) smoke on your clothing.

*During the interview for a new position, can I tell the
interviewer/HR director how difficult my current manager is
and why I need the new position?*
Absolutely not! Never speak negatively of anyone with whom
you have worked.

You are a participant in the interview process. You will answer
questions about yourself and discuss job-related topics, but the interview is also your opportunity to conduct your own interview of the
company representative. In general, prepare at least five good questions
about the company. You will show you have done some research and are
interested in the company.

- ❖ Ask about the company's future plans.
- ❖ Ask what types of people succeed at the company.
- ❖ Ask whether the position has potential for growth and where it
  might lead.
- ❖ Ask about areas of the company's business that you found par-
  ticularly interesting in your research.
- ❖ Ask if the company has a code of ethics.
- ❖ Ask if the company has an operations manual.
- ❖ Ask if the company has a dress code.
- ❖ Ask questions regarding the job description and about the
  specifics of the position in relation to other departments.

Just as the company is evaluating you during and after your interview, you need to be evaluating them. Did the interview begin on time?
Did the interviewer answer your questions or was she vague or evasive?
Did they ask you appropriate job-related questions and seem interested in
you? What was the reaction of the interviewer when you asked questions
from a list? If you asked questions on the annual report, what kind of responses did you receive? You have a responsibility to determine if this is a
company you will be able to support and work for. For instance, if you find
that your personal values and beliefs are not in alignment with what you
perceive to be the company's values, or you know that you do not perform
well within their management style, you may not want to work there.

Before you accept new responsibilities or a new job, review your own internal values, expectations, and desires. Employers are looking for individuals who are committed to the improvement and production of the company. Employees should consider their family responsibilities and take only those work assignments that enable and allow them to fulfill their commitments to their family. Family discussions about job commitment may be essential to keep the family intact. New job responsibilities, which create new stress and strains on the family, contribute to strained relationships. Discussion among the family members and understanding how you can balance your job demands with family commitments is critical to having a whole and productive person both at home and at the office.

Interview Follow-Up

Proper etiquette indicates that a thank you note should be sent immediately after the interview. Acknowledge the interviewer's time and the information you gained about the company during the interview and express your interest in working with the company. Even if you have concluded that the job or corporation is not a good match for you or your skills, send the thank you. Your graciousness will be remembered.

If you ask during the interview when the final hiring decision will be made, you may call at the agreed upon time and ask about the position. If you seriously thought you would get the job and were not selected, you may ask one of the interviewers for their suggestions about how you might better present your work experience and improve your interviewing skills. Also ask for suggestions about other positions within the corporation and any opportunities that might exist. Always be gracious and accept the suggestions even if they are critical or negative. Thank the person for their feedback.

ADVANCING YOUR CAREER

Moving up the career ladder involves the constant improvement of one's existing skills and the ability to learn new skills and put them into practice. Personal relationships are vital to business success; they are also important to your personal success in the workplace. You will have many opportunities to network and meet new people. Most people change jobs and even careers several times in the course of their work life. Developing new skills and accepting new responsibilities prepare you for these additional challenges and greater opportunities. Correct business etiquette will help move your career forward by demonstrating your professionalism and skills in working with and motivating others. Your ability to lead and influence others will further develop as you begin to manage a team and chair business meetings.

Networking

Networking is one of the most powerful business skills you can develop. When you use it well, you see the benefits. Once you start networking effectively, more than half of your business will come from referrals. The greatest business growth—obtaining information about jobs and meeting new people as prospective clients—comes as a result of successful networking. Networking is social marketing. Networking is about circulating at business functions on a social level. It is not about doing business per se, but about communicating. Networking involves our style of how we meet, greet, and keep in touch with our business colleagues.

Another definition of networking is the building of relationships through keeping in contact. This kind of networking is sometimes called self-marketing. We are always in the business of selling our skills, expertise, company, product, service, and competency.

Networking can be directly linked to promotion, advances, new jobs, new clients and, perhaps, even changing jobs. Networking, in brief, is meeting people, getting to know them, and keeping in touch. Never underestimate the power of networking. Think of the formula of ten to the sixth power. Everyone knows ten people and they in turn know ten people and so on to the sixth time. There is a saying that you are never more than six people from where you want to be. For example, when you need to find a speaker for your next sales meeting, ask your friends. Each has a thought about a good speaker they have heard or knows someone who hires speakers or plans meetings and can put you in touch with a speaker. Everyone wants to be needed and helpful. Talk to your business colleagues; tell them what you're looking for, and you will be amazed how easily you can get what you need! Among the acquaintances, colleagues, and friends you ask, one will have the answer.

There is a flip side to this, of course. Truly successful networking is a function of reciprocation. Someone helps you; you help them in return. Always keep in mind who helped you get to where you are so that you can help them. Everyone appreciates assistance, recognition, and respect.

Networking means connecting. It is knowing where to go, how to make conversation, keeping in touch, helping someone, giving leads, and following up on leads. Networking, then, is about building and maintaining business relationships. It encompasses all the best attributes of being a friend, business associate, and colleague. It involves a personal commitment to being helpful. It involves giving your time, ideas, and help and expecting the same from others. The person to whom you gave the lead may not always be the person who directly reciprocates, but someone else will. Networking isn't always a direct exchange of help. Courtesy, respect, and acknowledgment go further than you can imagine or measure.

The saying, "What goes around comes around," is true. Your reputation can come around to embrace you or knock you down. You are the only one with the ability to make it happen. Years later your actions speak for and about you. People remember what you did to or for them. It has been estimated that the circle comes around every three to five years. Coincidentally, five years is the length of the business success cycle. The building and establishment of business success takes five years until fruition. Make certain that your business reputation is one of credibility and courtesy.

Where and how you network is a personal decision. You don't need to join all the clubs, organizations, and associations. Begin with one that has special personal or business interest for you and build your networking from there. One frequently finds oneself overcommitted. Being involved in more than you can reasonably participate in is unnecessary. Occasionally we need to assess our time and how we can best use it to serve our colleagues. Participate as a contributing member by serving on committees and as an officer, if your time allows. People will see you in a support or leadership position, and you will become better acquainted with the membership.

Networking Opportunities

- ❖ Local chamber of commerce
- ❖ Service organizations such as Rotary International or Soroptimists
- ❖ Leads groups
- ❖ Business clubs and associations
- ❖ Trade organizations
- ❖ Social clubs
- ❖ Special-interest clubs (outdoors, biking, hiking, crafts, computer users)
- ❖ College classes
- ❖ Local charity involvement
- ❖ Local fund-raisers

Follow-up or "keeping in touch" is an essential aspect of networking. Keeping in touch reinforces the desire for acknowledgment, respect, and being needed. A friendly telephone call, note, or e-mail message are ways to acknowledge your contacts and put your name in front of them. Newsletters are great connectors because they impart information and remind others of your capabilities. A contact management computer program, a tickler file system, folders, file cards, or any other system can help you keep in touch with colleagues.

When I have a question or a need I tend to go to the people whose newsletter, card, or phone call has passed my desk recently. Networking involves frequent contact to keep your name and skills foremost in others' thoughts.

Working a Room

Working a room is a networking skill involving how you move about a room to make the most contacts and best use of your time. Sometimes we refer to networking or working a room as the way in which we move within a group of people to benefit and build business. Working a room can be fun or it can be intimidating. Many people dislike entering a room of strangers and finding someone and something to talk about. Practice moving about the room making contacts and being comfortable while gathering information, building new business associations, making business contacts, getting known, and having fun. The two keys to successfully working a room are planning and preparation.

If you are required to attend an event because the boss decided you were the best one to represent the company, mark your calendar and get ready. Establish goals for attending the event. This involves several of the business tools you need every day: business cards, a ready smile, interesting conversation topics, a concise self-introduction, and a goal. It is easier to work a room when you have a purpose such as to meet five new people, to find a graphic artist, or to meet a product supplier. Purpose helps you focus your efforts.

Plan your wardrobe well in advance so that you have appropriate clothing for the occasion with easily accessible pockets, an interesting accessory to make you memorable (necktie, vest, brooch, scarf), polished shoes, well-groomed hands and hair, and a smile. It helps to have an "in" pocket for the business cards you are given and an "out" pocket for your own business cards. Having the out pocket on the right side is easier because you can shake hands and immediately have a card ready to offer.

Where do you put your nametag?

A nametag is put on the right shoulder where it can be readily seen. The nametag's purpose is to reinforce your name. When you meet someone and shake hands, their gaze will automatically follow your right arm up to your shoulder and then to your face. Place the nametag high enough on your right shoulder to be easily seen.

Keep your hands as free as possible. Avoid carrying heavy items such as a handbag, shoulder bag, briefcase, or folders. Hold food in your left hand to keep your right hand free for hand shaking. If you are in a setting where there are appetizers or other nibbling types of food to eat and beverages to drink as you circulate, feel free to partake. Just remember it is difficult to balance both a glass and a plate. Eating minimally or not at all is recommended at a business networking event because your purpose is not to eat, it's to circulate.

Some behaviors can undermine even your best networking efforts. For best results avoid drinking more than one glass of any alcoholic beverage. Be careful not to eat, drink, and talk all at the same time. Monopolizing one individual or group of people will keep you from meeting others and may annoy those monopolized. Complaining about almost any subject, but especially about the room, food, or attendees will leave a negative impression with those you meet.

Networking is an opportunity to meet people and sell your business and services. Be careful not to push your business too hard as you may alienate more people than you impress. I met a man who had such a polished self-introduction that it was a huge turnoff. He was excited about his multilevel marketing program. His introduction was an invitation to join him and make lots of money and on and on he went with the dates of the next meetings and other information. In the few seconds he spoke, he alienated people all over the room! People avoided talking to him after his introduction because it sounded canned and phony. That reaction carries into perceived ideas about how you do business.

To successfully network a room you need to Plan, Prepare, and Participate.

Plan

- ❖ Mark your calendar.
- ❖ Develop your purpose.
- ❖ Select your clothing.
- ❖ Plan your self-introduction.
- ❖ Replenish your business card supply.

Prepare

- ❖ Scan newspapers and magazines to prepare interesting conversation topics.
- ❖ Prepare your small talk topics.

Since conversation is critical in making the networking connection, it is beneficial to prepare topics to talk about. These topics benefit you in any conversation. Your skill at conversation demonstrates that you are not one dimensional about your career.

To identify and learn more about topics for conversation, read at least one newspaper each day. Clip and collect articles that interest you. Read newsletters, professional journals, and periodicals of interest to you. Take note of interesting comments, stories, and quotes. Read book and movie reviews. It will also be helpful if you are knowledgeable about community happenings. Most people enjoy humor; use humor that is appropriate, tasteful, and timely.

❖ Review how to make proper introductions. (See Chapter 1, *The First Impression*.)

❖ Review and practice your self-introduction. (See Chapter 1, *The First Impression*.)

❖ Learn about the sponsor organization and/or purpose of the event.

Participate

❖ Enter the room with poise and confidence.

❖ Orient yourself to the room. Look for interesting people.

❖ Seek out people who appear uncomfortable or are standing alone. They will welcome your conversation and may be good business contacts as well.

❖ Make the most of nametags. Use people's names to greet them and start conversations.

❖ Deliver your conversation opener with a smile.

❖ Manifest a positive attitude.

❖ Move in and out of conversations.

❖ Ask questions of others.

❖ Ask for business cards from those you want to contact.

❖ Stand tall.

❖ Smile.

❖ Listen and pay attention. Use eye contact.

Develop active listening skills. Listening actively involves providing feedback as the other person speaks. Nod in agreement, maintain eye contact, comment, and repeat key points that the person makes so he will know you are listening closely.

Follow Up

* Deliver what you have promised (i.e., send the article, brochure, reference).
* Write a note of acknowledgment.
* Write notes on the business card: reference to date and place of meeting and any particular notes about the person.

Good manners are especially good business when you are working a room. Remember to make introductions, use people's names when speaking with them, hand out business cards appropriate to your business and conversations, and always be courteous and respectful of others. Wear appropriate clothing for the event so you look your best. First impressions are important.

Business Card Etiquette

* Cards should not be given to senior executives you meet (unless a card is asked for).
* Cards are given at the beginning of a meeting.
* Your card is not generally given at the beginning of the conversation when networking.
* Avoid scattering your cards in a large group or on a meeting table.
* Give your card when you are asked for one, when you are asked to repeat your name, or when someone offers to send you something.
* Be discerning about when to personalize your cards by writing on them.
* Always carry business cards. Carry them in a case to keep them neat.
* Ask for someone's card if you wish to get in touch with them.

Avoid writing on the face of someone's card in the presence of the giver because it could offend them. Take an opportunity when you are back at the office or in the privacy or your car or elsewhere to make notes on the cards. Write the date, where you met and any personal notes that will help to enhance future conversations, for example, wears hats, wears bow ties, plays golf, has a son in college. A brief comment about a person's interests may serve to later demonstrate your personal attention. It is the acknowledgment that makes the connection stronger. For example, a woman called my office and asked if I remembered her. I referred to my notes and commented where and when I met her. She was surprised and pleased that I remembered her!

I have a banker's card as a sample of what not to do. We were discussing business over tea and I asked for his card. He looked in his wallet and found only one card. You know, the last one seems to be the soiled one! He insisted that I take it despite my suggestion that he send me one when he returned to his office. He turned the card over to find a joke he had jotted down. He read the joke, laughed, and quickly crossed it off with his pen. Then he gave the card to me. Three years later, I still have the card and chuckle. I always forget his name but not his bank. I hesitate to invest my money in his bank or any of their community projects since his card is a strong reminder of how I perceive the bank to handle money. I think he may handle my money and our relationship the way he handled his card, without much care. My perception may not be the reality, but perception is the determinate of how we relate to others.

Managing a Team

Integrity and respect are major keys to successful management. Often we are thrust into a management position even though it's not part of the original job description or when we least expect it. One definition of management is aiding each member of the team in such a way that their performance enhances and moves the team to the stated objective. The key issue is to manage others as you would want to be managed. Helping each person, as you would want to be helped, is the mark of a good manager. If you need help in managing skills, inquire if there is management training available. Ask human resources about any seminars coming into the area that you might attend. If outside training is not available, look around the office and find a person whom you admire. Observe their management style. Ask questions and observe them working with their team. Emulate that style with your own team, then add your personal touch.

> *A good manager acknowledges, respects, guides, instructs, leads, and communicates; involves the team members in projects, successes, and planning; and shares the credit for work well done.*

Your first team assignment may be to solve a problem or establish a new program or project. Ask the team members for their ideas to resolve an issue or solve the problem. They will respect you for asking for their input and will work more diligently to achieve the goal. Ownership of the assignment comes from being acknowledged for contributing and from being asked for views and suggestions.

As a manager, do not ask for suggestions about how you might improve your management skills, especially at a staff meeting. You may be inviting an employee to lash out at you for reasons unrelated to your performance. It also leaves you vulnerable for others to attack you personally. Instead, ask for suggestions about how to get the job done more efficiently. Use phrases such as

- ❖ "How can the company . . . ?"
- ❖ "How can our team work better together?"
- ❖ "How can our team . . . ?"

Be prepared to modify remarks to avoid personal comments about another team members.

Every manager brings her own style to the management position. Your personal style of management is evident when your team is assembled. Guidelines for managing are the core, flavored with your personal style of conducting business.

In general, management and staff work better when they do not mix their business and personal lives. Whatever you discuss with one of your staff outside the workplace could easily become fodder for gossip in the workplace and may undermine your management position with the entire staff.

Chairing a Meeting

Have you refused to be chair for a meeting because you did not feel comfortable or qualified? Next time, consider taking the assignment and follow these suggestions. Like any other business meeting, you need to plan and prepare for it. Courteous consideration to the details will make the meeting run smoothly and help you feel more confident about directing the progress of the meeting and completing the agenda.

Every aspect of your professionalism is evident in your association with others whether you are conducting a meeting or managing a team. The emphasis is on efficiency in completing the project while at the same time demonstrating your respect for other people, their ideas, and their work. Your colleagues are your assets, and how you relate to them affects how they work with you. The chair's challenge is to make the meeting effective and efficient.

You can effectively accomplish your meeting goals by spending time to prepare before the meeting. You will need to plan the time and length of the meeting. The meeting agenda demands careful preparation. You will need to plan the subjects for the agenda and determine a specific number of minutes for each item. Distribute the agenda the day before the meeting and ask for suggestions on additional agenda items. Amend the agenda if new items are added.

Send brief reminder memos the day before the meeting with the following details:

- ❖ Time of meeting
- ❖ Location of meeting
- ❖ Discussion items

If you are chairing the meeting, take time the day before to plan what you will wear. If you will be seated for most of the meeting, others will only see you from the waist up. Select an interesting necktie, scarf, jewelry, and colors that will "attract" the eyes of the attendees. You want to have their attention.

On the meeting day, check the room fifteen minutes before the meeting begins. Take this opportunity to arrange chairs and make sure that there are enough chairs for your attendees. If you want a specific seating arrangement, set out name cards. For name cards, use tents with the name on both sides, so others seated at the table can see the name. As the chairperson, you may select your place at the table and indicate it by placing your own name placard, book, or a folder there. A briefcase or handbag may be placed on the chair seat. It is also thoughtful to provide water, glasses, napkins, paper, and pencils for the attendees, especially if the meeting is expected to last more than two hours.

The chair should arrive at the meeting early to make sure that everything is ready. An agenda should be distributed to every seat. As the chairperson, a part of your responsibility is to direct the meeting. You should begin on time or within five minutes of your scheduled start time. You may want to assign someone to take notes or arrange in advance for a staff person not participating in the meeting to take notes. Have an easily readable clock on the table in front of you, or face the wall clock if there is one. When you open the meeting, introduce yourself and ask each person to introduce themselves in one or two sentences. Make a concentrated effort to follow your agenda. Close the meeting on time even if all the items were not discussed.

Though you may feel that you have not accomplished the task, it is better to be prompt and end on time rather than to drag out the meeting for the sake of completing the agenda. Your attendees will be more willing to come to another meeting if you begin and end when you say you will. This applies to board meetings, staff meetings, brainstorming sessions, and association and club meetings. Your staff and colleagues are busy and will appreciate your ending the meeting on time. They have allowed time from their own work schedules to attend your meeting and may have other time commitments.

Is it appropriate to pay transportation or parking expenses for the attendees at my business meeting?

The attendees had the options not to attend or to submit their travel/parking expenses to the company. You are not responsible to pay their expenses. If your attendees must take public transportation or drive to a meeting and there is no expense reimbursement for travel, it is not imperative for you to pay their expenses, but it is a courtesy. You will find that your colleagues will be more eager to attend when they do not have to pay out-of-pocket to attend your meeting.

Should I pay my client's parking fine issued during our meeting?

Not necessarily. You may feel that they should have been mindful, and they might think that your meeting was too long. The decision depends on you and your relationship to the attendee. It is a courteous gesture to offer to pay. Depending on the amount of the fine, you could split the cost.

On the day after the meeting, send each attendee a synopsis of what was covered in the meeting and what was accomplished. You may even begin to plan the agenda items for the next meeting.

If you are the president or are chairing a board or chapter, then you must lead the meetings. Normally there is a president's book, which includes the order of conducting a meeting. If there is none, purchase *Robert's Rules of Order. Robert's Rules of Order* is the standard, universally accepted meeting procedure, and it details the order in which items are introduced during a meeting. Write out the format, put it under a plastic page protector, and add self-stick reminder notes of details for each meeting. You will have specific notes for each meeting that you can remove, move around, and discard after the meeting.

Serving as president or chair can be a rewarding experience. All you need is confidence to stand before a group and know how to set the meeting agenda and facilitate the meeting. Of course, you will need to exercise appropriate skills to close long or frivolous discussion about subjects that digress from the agenda items. If a member will be giving a report, speak to that person before the meeting day and suggest a specific time limit for the report.

If there is no precedent for a meeting procedure or agenda, or there is no meeting outline book for the president or chair, plan and prepare one for yourself that you can pass on to the succeeding chair. The next chair will appreciate it, and you will have contributed to the more efficient leadership of the group.

You might want to put the meeting format on your computer and fill it in for each meeting. A format can be developed with generic information and space for the specifics of each meeting. The date, time, agenda, and officers could even be on the form prior to the meeting.

Any time you can make the job easier, more efficient, and less threatening, you encourage volunteers to help. Simplifying a job often attracts willing helpers.

When You Attend a Meeting

Attendees also have responsibilities when attending a meeting. Prepare yourself for the meeting by familiarizing yourself with the meeting agenda. Review the items and be prepared to contribute your ideas. Arrive at the meeting on time. You make a poor impression when you arrive at a meeting that is already in progress. Select a seat where you can see well and make your voice heard.

The ability to chair a meeting and to lead others, as in managing a team, are skills vital to success in today's business world. As business becomes more highly technical and we work with more electronic tools, it's easy to forget about developing our interpersonal skills, skills that are more important than ever. Our fellow employees and our clients all thrive when they feel respected and cared for. Knowing proper business etiquette will give you the confidence to act and to lead effectively with grace and style.

Chapter 8

Office Finesse

$\mathcal{T}$he office reflects the organization of the company and the ethics and values important to the corporate culture. Companies can leave a positive or negative impression on visitors or clients, just as individuals can. Often this impression is made as soon as the visitor enters the office.

RECEPTION

Whether you are the receptionist or the first person to greet a visitor to your office you have a responsibility to make that visitor feel at ease. You should stop what you are doing and acknowledge the visitor with eye contact and a smile. If you are on the phone, a nod with eye contact acknowledges the visitor and helps them feel welcome. As soon as possible, greet the visitor verbally. Visitors who are clients or potential customers are not an interruption of your work, but the reason you have work. Give a few minutes of your time to make office visitors feel comfortable and to notify the person with whom the visitor has an appointment.

It is important to provide a pleasant atmosphere in your waiting area. If they are available, offer refreshments such as coffee, tea, water, or soda. Let the visitor know where the rest rooms are located so they don't have to ask. Offer to take overcoats to a closet or have a visible place where visitors may hang their own coats. Chairs in the waiting area should be comfortable and easy to get in and out of. The company should also provide interesting reading material, company brochures, or current news and trade magazines. Always remember that the waiting area or lobby of your office is an extension of the office and a place of business.

Etiquette for the Receptionist

The receptionist does not normally shake hands with clients or other visitors to the office. If you have the appointment schedule at your desk, speak to the person by name with a title such as Ms. or Mr. If you are unsure of their name you may ask gently for their name and with whom they have an appointment. You should then introduce yourself using your full name. You may ask for a business card if the visitor hasn't offered one to you. You will then have their correct name and the company they represent.

As the receptionist, there are many additional things you can do to make your visitors feel welcome. You may anticipate their needs by being observant of their body language and actions. This is a skill that can be developed with time and practice. You may wish to offer assistance on public transportation or obtaining telephone numbers if necessary.

Greeting guests is an important responsibility. The lobby is the first area where a visitor has an opportunity to observe your business at work. They are forming an impression of your company while they wait. To help make a positive impression, avoid personal phone conversations or talking about others who work in your office. Do not make comments about other clients or suppliers. Refrain from personal grooming, such as filing nails or combing hair.

The receptionist is not responsible for entertaining visitors while they wait. Keep verbal responses to a visitor's inquiries friendly, yet tactful and succinct.

When you are ready to show the visitor to another office, tell them "Ms. Jones is ready to see you, let me show you (with a gesture) to the meeting room." Avoid command statements such as "Follow me" or "Come with me." When you arrive at the office or meeting room, hand the business card to Ms. Jones, make the proper introduction, and excuse yourself from the room, unless you have been asked to remain and take notes.

Etiquette for Greeting Your Visitor Personally

Many companies do not have a receptionist to greet guests so you may be greeting the visitor yourself. If the lobby security has notified you that your visitor has arrived, you can be waiting at the elevator. Even if you have not previously met the person, you can assume when someone steps from the elevator that he is your guest, and you can step forward to greet them. If the person is not your visitor or client, you have an opportunity to help them locate the individual they have come to see. If the visitor has been to your offices before, you need not go to the elevator or reception for each visit, though it is an appreciated courtesy.

If your schedule keeps your visitor waiting more than ten minutes past the appointed meeting time, personally go out and greet them or notify your receptionist that you will be delayed another ten minutes. Avoid keeping your visitor waiting more than twenty minutes. Likewise, if you are the visitor you should not be more than ten minutes late without calling the office to apprise them of your expected arrival.

Every time you enter a room you are noticed. Your body language, gestures, grooming, and personal style set the tone for the meeting. Always be cognizant of how others perceive you. It is essential to maintain professionalism with your personal style. You can be friendly and fun, but remain professional; the balance of the two is yours to create.

GREETING DIVERSE INDIVIDUALS

Each of us brings our uniqueness and personal talents to the workplace. Our work skills can fit well together for the benefit of all when we are tolerant of our differences and makes allowances for the faults, opinions, and habits of others.

Corporate policy extends to how diversity is handled in the front office as well as on the production line. A challenge for the business person is understanding diversity and being able to select and train those who work in the business. Diversity is not just about ethnicity, but about understanding people. It encompasses all the different backgrounds and educational experiences that people bring to their work. Our work environment must be a place of cooperation and understanding.

Tolerance works two ways: you must be tolerant of the beliefs of others, others must be tolerant of your beliefs. While you are free to follow religious or philosophical beliefs different from others, you are not free to impose your beliefs on everyone around you. Tolerance of other's beliefs is critical in creating a comfortable work environment.

We all want to enjoy personal freedoms but we must also be aware of the responsibility we have to others. For instance, having the freedom to decorate your work area is fine but you must be willing to accept guidelines as to what is appropriate. Good sense, decency, and courtesy are key considerations.

Second Languages

Employees and clients all may benefit from knowing more than one language, particularly because we work and live with people from many backgrounds and parts of the world. It is not impossible to learn another language as an adult, though more difficult than as a child. Many businesses are marketing their products to international markets and ethnic groups. If your company engages in international business, study the culture and language of that region. If you have the privilege of parents and relatives who speak a second language, learn from them. It will enhance not only your language skills, but also your understanding of the differences and similarities that exist between peoples.

When you greet visitors who speak a different language or who are bilingual, be patient and do your best to assist them. You don't need to speak louder if they don't understand you; they can usually hear you just fine. Speak slowly, and use simple language if that is easier for them to understand.

Physical Disabilities

Diversity extends to dealing with people with disabilities. Laws have required businesses to accommodate wheelchairs at entrances and rest rooms as well as provide access within the buildings. Disabled individuals lead active and productive lives and you will, no doubt, need to greet and work with many individuals with disabilities of one kind or another in the course of your business career.

Many people have asked what the proper way to shake hands with someone who has lost a right hand. Instead of greeting by shaking hands, the greeting is made by touching. You may lay a hand on the wrist, forearm, or shoulder; you should always smile, just as you would if you were actually shaking hands. If you see that the right hand is disfigured due to an accident, arthritis, or a splint or cast, touch the hand lightly.

If you are unsure what to do, be respectful and acknowledge the individual in some other way. Sometimes, they will guide you. If you have the damaged hand extend your hand or arm to indicate how you would like to be greeted. You can ease the awkwardness others feel. Most nondisabled do not know how to reach out to you and will be eager to learn.

Some specific suggestions when working with disabled colleagues and employees follow.

Wheelchair-Bound

When speaking to a person in a wheelchair, sit in a chair or kneel so that you will be closer to the same eye level. Don't make the wheelchair-bound person look up at you for the duration of the conversation. Avoid leaning on their chair or bumping it.

Some disabled persons have limited mobility but can move from their wheelchair to a standard seat. When the disabled person is seated in a standard chair, place their wheelchair (or crutches or cane) near them.

Ask if you may push the wheelchair before doing so. Some people on wheels value their freedom to move on their own, without assistance, while others will appreciate your help.

Hearing-Impaired

Get the person's attention so they are looking at you. Some hearing-impaired individuals can read lips or can understand much of what you say as long as they can see your face. If you turn your face away while you are speaking, they may not understand that part of what you have said. For instance, if you gesture toward the blackboard and turn your face toward it while still talking, the hearing-impaired person will not be able to see your face and may not "hear" what you said. You'll also want to speak clearly and slowly, without shouting.

Visually-Impaired

The visually-impaired may be completely blind or have only partial blindness. Some visually-impaired individuals use a white cane, others have a canine companion. When you greet a visually-impaired individual, face the person and speak clearly. Introduce yourself so she will know who is talking with her. You may make physical contact on the arm.

Some blind persons have a canine companion. This animal is often the most important and comforting companion the disabled person has and is loved unconditionally. The natural inclination is to admire, speak to, and pet this specially trained dog. It is thoughtful to verbally acknowledge the seeing-eye dog, perhaps ask what its name is, ask permission to pet it (if you desire to), and make other appropriate comments. Without permission, do not distract the "working dog."

Many visually-impaired people hear remarkably well and perhaps even better than their sighted colleagues do. Speak to them as you would a sighted person, using proper etiquette. Speak at a normal level and enunciate your words well.

I spoke recently with a visually-impaired person about his dog and his work. In the course of our conversation, he shared with me that the most annoying thing that sighted people do is not look at him. Even though his eyes weave and he doesn't see, he has such acute hearing that he knows when the person is facing him, doing something else while speaking to him, or seems to be otherwise distracted. Imagine the kind of negative impression these sighted individuals are leaving on this man. Practicing good manners is just as important in working with the disabled as with other individuals.

When you walk with a visually-impaired person, ask the person if they would like to take your arm. If you have never walked with a visually-impaired person before, tell them so, and ask for their help. Ask them if you should warn them about steps or other obstacles. Frequently, they can tell when you step down if they are holding your arm, and follow along accordingly. Whenever you are nearby, announce your presence. If you leave the room, let them know. If others come in, introduce the visually-impaired person as you would other visitors.

Speech-Impaired

Individuals with speech impairments have difficulties in saying words. You will need to be patient and extra attentive with these individuals and resist the temptation to finish their sentences or thoughts for them. They may need a little more time to express themselves, but their ideas are nonetheless valuable. You can help by asking questions that only require brief answers and by speaking slowly and clearly yourself.

Developmentally-Challenged

Developmentally-challenged individuals may be both mentally and/or physically slower than average. Depending on the severity of their "challenge" you may need to repeat yourself several times, particularly if you are giving instructions to perform a task. It is especially important to exercise patience and to listen carefully. Their speech may be hesitant or difficult to comprehend. These people are very sensitive and want to be independent, so speaking in simple short sentences eases communication. All people desire respect and acknowledgment. You may need to repeat and even restate your comments and questions. Do not talk down to them no matter what developmental age they appear to be. Laughter eases tension and frustration, and smiling goes a long way to make others feel more comfortable.

In General

Always demonstrate patience with the disabled. You may want to allow extra time for your meetings with the physically disabled so they will not feel rushed. Smile, be gracious, show respect, and give them dignity. If your company has clients with special needs, take that into consideration when arranging offices and reception areas.

There are tax benefits for businesses that hire special needs people. You may have the opportunity to work with and train a physically challenged person somewhere in your career. Perhaps your client will be a Ph.D. with a speech disability. If your office has physically challenged employees or clients with special needs, consider modifying the walking space, traffic patterns, and seating in your office to more easily accommodate them. An added courtesy is to keep lightweight, large-handled mugs in the employee lounge.

ROMANCE IN THE OFFICE

A growing number of individuals from corporate offices to coffee shops are finding romance in the workplace. Today's emphasis on teamwork and longer work hours make the work environment an opportunity for personal relationships. Today's busy, almost frantic, and often stressful lifestyle does not allow much free time for meeting interesting people outside the office. With a huge portion of our lives devoted to business, meetings, and associated activities, the likelihood of meeting someone we might wish to date is highly possible.

> *I am looking for my soul mate. Shall I look through the company to find her?*
>
> *If I meet a coworker I would like to know better, can we date?*
>
> *What should I do if someone in the office keeps suggesting we go out, and I do not want to go?*

These are reasonable questions, that arise because we all spend so much of our time in the workplace. If the answers were easy, we wouldn't need to address them here. Situations differ from office to office; you must exercise good judgment and follow company policy, if there is one.

There are special considerations when romance occurs in the office or at work related activities. The office seems like a favorable setting for relationships because you can see that special person every day, you share common interests, and you have opportunities to get to know one another in a familiar setting. It also seems appealing because your time is so limited to meet others outside of work. Beware, romance in the workplace could destroy your career. The problems that may occur are not always apparent or anticipated at the onset of a romantic relationship but the results may be lower productivity, damaging gossip, loss of job, and career derailment.

Many companies discourage office romance because they are concerned with loss of productivity. Seeing one another frequently during work, spending excessive time on breaks, consulting with one another too often, one helping the other inappropriately, and spending time solving personal problems interferes with work. When at work, your attention should be on getting the job done without the override of personal problems. Just as bill paying and personal phone calls should be reserved for break time and after hours, so should romantic or intimate relations.

The old adage of not mixing work and personal life is coming under new scrutiny. Corporate travel, long hours in luxury hotels, late night work, and weekends are contributors not just to short-term flings, but to longer liaisons as well. Although interoffice relationships are gaining wider acceptance among employees, interoffice romances are still fraught with danger.

If you find that a coworker is touching your heartstrings, give careful consideration to the future of your job and career. Office romance can create competition for promotions or put you in a compromising position. For instance, it would be difficult to resolve the conflict of interest that would arise if one of you were in a position to impact the other's career. Do you place your loyalty and responsibility with your employer or your love interest? In addition, you must each be able to trust that the other will not reveal personal information to fellow employees or supervisors. It can be difficult to nurture a relationship when there is fear about repercussions when things go wrong. You will need a plan and a strategy to keep work and romance separate.

It is essential that you keep the relationship discreet; this can be quite a challenge. Any meeting during the workday must be private, brief, and without obviously romantic overtones.

Romance in the workplace has caused tremendous concern for companies and is even forbidden in some companies. Many companies have nepotism policies that prohibit employment of spouses or other relatives in order to avoid any accusation of favoritism to relatives, especially in promotions. Some companies require that the two individuals work at separate office locations or in different branches of the company. If your relationship is long term or you are married, one of you may be required to leave the company.

Check your company's policy before entering into a relationship at work or at least before the relationship becomes public, which it inevitably will. Companies are seriously concerned about loss of productivity and problems that might occur if the relationship goes sour. Companies also fear sexual harassment lawsuits that may arise when workplace affairs go wrong.

If you meet the "right person" and begin a romantic relationship, check the company policy. As much as possible, it is best to avoid romantic associations with others sharing your workspace, with those who have similar work responsibilities, or with individuals of lower corporate stature, as when the vice president of marketing is dating the company receptionist. You should also avoid romantic associations with those whom you see regularly at work.

Corporate policies can be established to provide guidelines for romance in the workplace. If they are not written where you work, inquire as to any unwritten policy. Regardless of how strongly you are attracted to a coworker, think about the consequences to both of your future careers.

Romance in the customer/client area can also be sticky. Being romantically linked with a client may seem reasonable but again, beware. Will job productivity suffer? Are you getting your job done effectively? Is the relationship with the client still profitable for the company? Being linked to a client romantically can lead to gossip, resentment about possible favors, demands for extra corporate perks or other considerations, and expectations beyond the normal company/client relationship. Check your corporate policy, if there is one, discreetly consult with a supervisor, and be mindful of the possible implications for your future.

CULTURAL COURTESY

Everyone dealing in today's global markets is touched by cultural diversity. Knowing what to do and having an understanding of cultural differences eases the way to a long and profitable business association. When traveling abroad or meeting foreign guests, be aware of cultural considerations that can make a difference in your business relationship. Learn a few words in your foreign guest's language if you want to change your reception from cool to cordial. Visitors almost always appreciate that you've taken some effort to make them feel welcome and comfortable.

You'll also need to understand any gestures or topics of conversation that should be avoided. You may ask about children, but not about a spouse. Avoid talking about religion or the politics of their country. Knowing the names of the country's leaders is appropriate. Many cultures follow formal protocols, both in business and in their daily lives. For instance, careful considerations may be necessary in planning seating arrangements at meetings to show your respect for their more formal ways. For instance, the number of seats at the table and the time of day for the meeting may be important.

In general, when working with foreign visitors,

- ❖ Speak and act in a formal way. Avoid profanity or language that is overly friendly, as it may be perceived as inappropriately familiar.

- ❖ Know and use titles. Be especially careful not to use first names unless you are invited to do so; address visitors as Mr. or Ms. if there is no other title.

- ❖ Know and pronounce names correctly. This may take some practice when names are unusual or unfamiliar; repeat the names when you are introduced.

- ❖ Be punctual. Tardiness is very inconsiderate.

- ❖ Dress conservatively. Avoid flashy clothing and jewelry that may not be appropriate. Practice good grooming habits.

Gifting practices also vary; some cultures have protocols for accepting and giving gifts and strict guidelines as to appropriate gifts. The Japanese value gift wrapping and expense of the gift. Gifts to Asian peoples should never consist of four items, as that is symbolic of death in their tradition. Easily transported gifts of fine chocolates, local edible products, coffees and teas, and regional items make appropriate gifts.

Dietary customs also vary in other cultures and in other religions. You'll need to know if your guests are observing a fast, during which they do not eat for a set period of time, often in observance of religious belief and sometimes for other purposes as well. You'll also need to know if your visitor observes any dietary restrictions. Many people also avoid certain foods; beware of preferences in selecting the places where you will be dining. This will be particularly important if you are planning a business meal. Dining times vary by country.

Know the holidays, religion, and government of your guests. A friend once had an English client who became very concerned when he couldn't reach their office for several days one November. It was Thanksgiving, a strictly American holiday, and he wasn't aware of it! Your guests may observe religious or other significant days of which you are not currently aware.

In your conversation, avoid comparing one country with another. In fact, avoid criticism of any country. Your guest may find your comments offensive or uninformed. In any case, they may conclude that you are quick to make judgments about others. Humorous jokes often fail to translate well and should be avoided. Every culture has its own appreciation of humor.

While with your guests, avoid showing lots of money or large bills and avoid casual remarks about money. Many cultures are sensitive about these issues for one reason or another. Current exchange rates also tend to fluctuate somewhat and may be a cause of concern.

WOMEN IN THE WORKPLACE

Women are reaching higher levels of management and accepting increased business responsibilities. Breaking through the glass ceiling continues to be a difficult and ongoing battle. Women are overcoming obstacles and making progress by bringing their unique skills to the workplace and developing business ethics that complement their values.

These skills include the ability to compromise, to be calm, to listen intently, to search for win–win solutions, to focus, to be nurturing, to be supportive, and to be a leader. This is not to say that these skills are not present in men, they are not as recognizable. Men tend to appear more ruthless and cutthroat in business negotiations. Generally, winning is the game for men while win–win is totally acceptable to women.

Unfortunately, issues such as negativism, backbiting, and gossip continue to be as common among women in business as among their male counterparts. Sadly, some men and women who rise to the top begin to criticize others along the way, believing that by causing their coworkers to appear incompetent, they appear more competent. Women, by emulating their male counterparts, sometimes unknowingly often prevent other women from advancing in their careers. Because women bring the sensitivity and emotion to the workplace that is so often minimized in the male-dominated world, they would be well advised to actively make efforts to mentor others and to help them learn which skills to enhance and which actions to avoid to accelerate their career advancement.

Although it may be true that many women are content to work in supporting business roles and are satisfied being contributors, many are also striving to achieve increased responsibilities and strong leadership roles. Because it is so difficult to break through the glass ceiling, many women entrepreneurs are founding their own companies and thus are performing the strong leadership roles they desire and are becoming role models for women in the corporate world.

Misinformed women often compromise themselves by attempting to conduct business the way men do. Competition at the top is keen no matter what the gender, and if a woman conducts herself as men often do, she will often be brutally chastised by her male counterparts. Once a woman has broken through the glass ceiling, to be really successful she must continue to use her unique qualities. Women can make compromises in ways that do not affect their personal values, can play by the rules once they are defined, and be totally focused and professional without defaulting to defamatory criticism and comments. Women need to realize that their opinions are valuable, that they have as much right to express what they are thinking as anyone else, and that they have the required skills to perform any management function required. Women earn respect by being competent and fair in all their business activities.

What can women do better to make themselves credible? Learn to speak with authority. Be an expert on your subject without flaunting it. Be able to chair a meeting using *Robert's Rules of Order*. Keep meetings on track by addressing the issues and not succumbing to or participating in small talk. Dress conservatively, but with personal style, keeping in mind that you are selling your expertise, nothing else. Practice good grooming habits and make sure that your personal image is perfect when you arrive at the next business function.

Dressing professionally is an art. Clothes should be conservative but with personal style and good taste. There are personal consultants who can shop with you to get the right professional image. There are aestheticians who can help design a makeup ensemble that is professional and attractive. Women should use personal consultants, estheticians, manicurists, pedicurists, and other professional services so that they can always look their very best. When you know that you look great, you will exude confidence and your business role will reflect this confidence.

Gender and Etiquette

Gender has no place for issues of etiquette in the business world. The issues of etiquette around who opens a door, who assists whom, whether men stand up when women enter or leave a room, cause confusion. The basic rule to follow is that we are colleagues, and if someone needs assistance with a door, carrying packages, or whatever, offer assistance. Otherwise, as a thoughtful and courteous gesture, a man should open a door for a woman. If he doesn't, don't make an issue of it for men are often confused on whether they should help a woman in the "liberated" women's world. My belief is that women can be feminine and professional while accepting courtesies performed by men.

CUSTOMER SERVICE

Customer service is important to all aspects of doing business with your clients. Every client wants to be acknowledged, to feel respected, and to believe that his business is valued. Every contact with a customer is a form of customer service. Practicing good manners and proper etiquette is important to building and nurturing customer relationships.

When your client enters your office, you want him to be greeted cordially and to see a clean, attractive office; desks neat, furniture in good condition, clean floors, all with a comfortable, pleasant, and productive ambiance. You want the people working to look clean and well groomed, with clothing that is appropriate for the service, location, and place of work. Take a look at your office or business from your customer's viewpoint and see if there are changes you might consider.

❖ Is the entry lobby or waiting area pleasant and comfortable?

❖ Are desks and work surfaces neat, but not barren?

❖ Are there comfortable chairs for clients/customers to use?

❖ Does your receptionist face the entry door?

❖ Are clean rest rooms available for clients and workers?

❖ Is the background noise or music quiet and pleasant?

❖ Do employees appear to be appropriately dressed for their work?

Customer service is a key concept in today's business world. For good reason, customers have every right to expect service that is not only prompt and professional but also pleasant. When you know your clients well you can anticipate their needs. When you also know your product and deliver good service, your positive reputation grows, and customers will seek your business and services and refer others to you. The key factors for quality service and superior customer care are the following:

❖ Listen actively and ask questions to better understand what your customer needs.

❖ Offer more perceived value. Give more than the customer expects. You can offer to pay the shipping charges, include a return label for easy returns, offer free upgrades to software. You can make follow-up calls to check on customer satisfaction and send a thank you note after a large purchase. I work with a supplier who tosses a few pieces of hard wrapped candy into his packing material!

❖ When you speak with your clients, avoid using profanity, telling ethnic jokes, or using inappropriate humor. In participating in such conversations, you take a risk of leaving an unprofessional image.

❖ Return phone calls promptly. No one wants to feel ignored or that their concern is not important. Call to make sure your customer is happy with the services they received. Keep in touch with your clients so that as other needs arise, you'll be ready to deliver. You can also keep them apprised of new services you have to offer.

❖ Be visible. Your clients like you to see them and speak with them. The idea of knowing the owner or salesperson appeals to customers.

❖ Thank your client for her business and her input and feedback. To thank your client is more than just polite; it's good business.

Your customer is the reason you have a successful business. Service is what you have to offer to distinguish yourself from your competitors. Service your clients in ways to help them do their jobs better. Always strive to make every situation a win–win one. We are all in the business of service whether we are offering a product, management, or a production line. The ultimate goal is to have satisfied clients/customers. How can you best accomplish this? By giving the best of yourself to your business associates, colleagues, and clients, treating them with dignity and respect, helping them to do their job better, and delivering what you promise, both in product and in service.

Have you noticed how often we hear stories about poor service? It seems that one will tell others when they get good service, but they'll tell ten times as many people if they get poor service. Imagine the impact even one incident of poor service could have on your business. A neighbor purchased a new kitchen stove that he also had installed. Unfortunately, the stove wouldn't work properly. It took two service calls before the problem was determined to be a damaged part that had to be ordered from the manufacturer. He waited three weeks without any word from the store. He eventually called and no one seemed to know anything about the ordered part; they finally told him the order must have been lost, and they'd have to reorder it. Naturally, he was pretty unhappy. While he was waiting (and waiting) for them to repair the brand new stove, they sent an invoice marked overdue, which made him even more unhappy with the store and the way they treated him. He told me this story, just as he told every neighbor on the block. Word of mouth is such a powerful referral!

Your ability to convince your client that she is important to your company and that you will give her excellent service is what makes her happy to be a repeat customer and to refer friends to you. The manner in which you treat your customers with courteousness pays off with their business and their loyalty. Greeting customers with a smile, in person or on the phone, efficiently correcting any problems, and offering quality products will create trust and loyalty. When you succeed in making your customer feel important to your business, he will bring you repeat business and referrals.

Customer service is customer care. It is your expression of caring for your clients and their needs. When you bring new people into your business, make sure they understand the importance of your clients and their business. Always treat your client as though he is your best and only client.

THE HOME OFFICE

There are definite benefits to working at home. Foremost among them is the flexibility that comes from being able to set your own schedule and your own priorities. You also have no outside demands from coworkers, no dress code, and no set work hour schedule. You can walk the dog and care for the children.

The negative side of working at home is that you have no one to talk to (at the water cooler or copy machine) or consult with. Working at home can be lonely. It also requires self-discipline. It's easy to be distracted by the chocolate cake from last night, the project you started in the garage, or the letter you promised Aunt Matilda. You may also begin to forget about good manners and proper etiquette where they aren't necessarily on display all day. You'll need to keep your manners tool kit, that is, your etiquette skills, polished and ready to use, anytime you have dealings with the outside world, whether by phone, fax, e-mail, or by personal consultation from your home office. You can become lazy at home, thus practicing your etiquette skills at every opportunity is all the more important.

You may work at home because you run your own small business or you are part of a work-at-home program of a larger company. With the array of electronic office machines available, it is possible to be at home or even be in another part of the world and still be connected with the corporate offices.

Perhaps one of the greatest challenges of working at home is maintaining and promoting your own professional image. You can wear your pajamas and bunny slippers while conducting business and, of course, no one can see you. Are you aware, however, that the professionalism you project in your voice and your choice of words is based on what you are wearing and how you are sitting? Strange as it may sound, it is true. Most people act according to the way they are dressed. Think about how different you act when you are dressed appropriately for an important meeting as opposed to how you act when you are dressed to go out and mow the lawn or play tennis. You don't necessarily need to wear a business suit in your home office, but for best results you should be dressed in appropriate street clothes and sitting in a chair at a desk whenever you are working. Clothing you wear to work at home may not be adequate for outside meetings. Do you have a professional wardrobe for business meetings?

Working at home can create problems when you need to meet with clients or other visitors. Will you entertain visitors in your office? Do you have seating for them in your office, or will you use some other part of your home to meet? You may prefer to meet with clients in their place of business or over coffee at a local coffee shop, depending upon the nature of your business. Dining etiquette will take on a greater significance if most of your meetings involve dining settings. Are there other kinds of meeting places nearby? You'll also want to consider how you will handle mixed gender meetings and meetings with strangers in the relative privacy and seclusion of your home. Both you and your guest need to feel comfortable and safe no matter where you meet.

Keeping your home office or workspace organized will also help you to project the professional and competent image necessary for success. In your home office,

- ❖ Keep important business files readily accessible.
- ❖ Have a business phone line separate from your home phone line.

❖ Have a separate phone line for your computer (e-mail) and fax.

❖ Have a separate phone line for your fax if you have a separate fax machine and your business warrants one.

❖ Have a specific place for the laptop or computer.

❖ Have ample light in your office.

❖ Create a pleasant environment for yourself.

❖ Have adequate heat or air-conditioning to work comfortably.

❖ Minimize distractions from barking dogs and crying children.

Choosing to work at home brings other considerations as well. If you do not wish people to know where you live, establish a post office box as your mailing address. Depending upon the nature of your work and how many visitors you see in your office, you may need an outside entrance to your office. Others living in your home, such as your spouse, may not appreciate strangers traipsing through the living room and down the hall. Besides, most households have all kinds of activities in progress, many of which are not going to seem very professional. Have you wondered what your guest might think when they have to step over your daughter's naked Barbie doll?

When you work at home, you can also miss out on opportunities to network with colleagues and other business associates. Make plans to take an occasional business seminar or join a business club of some kind to further your professional growth. Be sure to practice proper etiquette at these functions to make the best impression possible. The person you meet may be your next client.

Chapter 9

Business Travel

$\mathcal{T}$oday's business demands often include travel. You may be attending business conferences, conducting product or services presentations in other cities, representing your company at trade shows, or personally building business relationships. You are traveling as a representative of your company; leave all you meet with a lasting and positive impression by using good manners and Power Etiquette. Whatever your reason for travel, plan your travel so that you are relaxed and ready to work when you reach your destination.

Begin by establishing an efficient way to make reservations. You may choose to use a travel agent who has all your personal travel preferences such as seat choice, time of day to travel, new city arrival time, hotel preference, and airline choice. You may make your own travel arrangements by using an on-line reservations site or you may call the airline directly.

Electronic (paperless) tickets are a popular alternative to standard tickets. You pick up your electronic tickets at the airport rather than wait for delivery by mail. Check with the airline regarding rules and restrictions. You may need to present a printed ticket receipt and a valid photo ID. Electronic tickets may be challenging to convert if a flight is cancelled and you need a flight on another airline.

Proper planning helps in making your travel arrangements and packing for the trip easier and more efficient. Baggage is easier to handle if you use a rolling 22- or 25-inch suitcase. There are a variety of styles and levels of quality available. Purchase the highest quality that you can afford. There are two convenient designs: one with a suit section and one with an open compartment with pockets. Either works well, but the suit section allows your jacket to be hung to reduce wrinkles.

Limits for carry-on baggage, as well as restrictions on their contents, vary among domestic and international airlines. Some domestic airlines allow two carry-on bags or one carry-on and one laptop computer. Check with your airline in advance to see how many carry-ons they currently allow; they will also be able to tell you the size limitations or other restrictions for your carry-on bags. International flights generally allow only one carry-on bag.

If you travel often keep a small bag with toiletries packed and in the suitcase. To avoid forgetting items or having empty containers, replenish the items when you return so that you are always ready for the next trip. For extra security, carry bottles with liquids in small resealable sandwich bags.

Items to Keep Ready for Travel

- ❖ Passport
- ❖ Toiletry kit with full containers
- ❖ Shoe polishing cloth and shoe bags
- ❖ Travel envelope for tickets and travel vouchers
- ❖ Money pouch for cash, credit cards, and valuables
- ❖ Business cards and company brochures
- ❖ Checklist of things to pack

Begin with the following checklist or develop your own.

- ☐ Toiletry kit with small containers
- ☐ Suit, shirt, and tie/blouse
- ☐ Shoes and hosiery/socks
- ☐ Extra pair of shoes
- ☐ Jacket and slacks to wear
- ☐ Accessories (neckties, jewelry, belts, scarves)
- ☐ Casual clothes
- ☐ Lightweight overcoat
- ☐ Umbrella

Select travel clothing that resists wrinkles and is comfortable. Your garment selection should include a high-quality suit that fits you well. Conservative color choice and style are essential for flexibility and long wearing. Pack a white shirt or blouse, conservative necktie/scarf, and appropriate jewelry. Travel in comfortable clothing that is wrinkle resistant and can be worn for casual meetings or sightseeing. Casual clothing, such as slacks and a jacket, collared shirt, and loafers are suitable travel clothes. You maintain your professional business look and also have comfort. Your luggage should contain your business attire with a spare shirt/blouse and extra slacks/skirt, shoes, and undergarments.

As you travel, keep detailed records and receipts for all expenses, including gratuities. As often as possible, pay your business expenses with a business credit card. Doing so will simplify reimbursement later.

When junior and senior executives travel together, the junior executive is responsible for ensuring that the travel arrangements are in order. The junior executive handles checking into the hotel on arrival and settling the bill at departure, tipping, and restaurant reservations. In other words, the junior executive handles all the travel details.

Business travel generally requires long hours and a fair amount of energy to maintain your stamina and professional astuteness. Be sure to reserve some time to take care of yourself. Plan time to exercise and relax by taking a walk in the fresh air, swimming, and/or having a massage or meditating. As glamorous as travel sounds, it is hard work, often more so than a normal work day at the office. When you are well rested, you are more likely to remember and practice proper business etiquette.

AUTOMOBILE AND LIMOUSINE ETIQUETTE

The limousine driver, or chauffeur, will open the curb side door for you and your guests when entering or leaving the limousine. Wait for him to do so. The host should enter the vehicle first so that guests do not have to slide across the seat, and so he can easily give instructions to the driver. If space inside is limited, the junior executive should sit in the jump seat, reserving the primary seat for the senior executive and his guest(s). If there is a bar, the host may offer the guests drinks if appropriate and if there is time before they will reach their destination. After giving the driver directions, the host may ask him to roll up the privacy window, if there is one. Limousine drivers should be tipped according to the time they've spent with you and the services provided. A trip across town in the hotel limousine should equal the cost of a cab covering the same route. A half day spent making stops for shopping or sightseeing, carrying packages, waiting at your meetings, running errands, or picking up guests at their hotel deserves a gratuity equal to the time and service. Gratuities may range from $10.00 to $100.00 depending upon the time and services. (Also see the *Gratuity Guide* in Chapter 3.)

When you are fortunate enough to have a limousine provided for your use, be careful not to abuse the privilege. It may not be at your disposal for shopping, sightseeing, or entertaining friends outside the company business. If the limousine is designated at your disposal for the duration of your stay in the city, coordinate with the driver and make special requests in advance.

When you are a passenger in another's vehicle and there are more than two passengers, ask where you should sit. Otherwise, assume you will sit next to the driver.

If traveling by taxi cab, the preferred passenger seat is on the rear passenger side. The junior person enters first and slides over, followed by the senior person, and guest if any. If a valet is assisting you, the host enters first to slide over. The guest, whether male or female, should not have to slide over. The driver side rear seat allows you to speak to the driver without speaking over the other passengers. This position also allows you to pay the driver since you will be the last passenger to leave the vehicle. Taxi cab drivers sometimes open doors for their passengers and sometimes do not. Be observant of courtesies and tip accordingly.

AIR TRAVEL

Travel by air is frequently the quickest way to get from a business meeting in one city to a conference in another. When traveling by air, you may choose from coach class, first class, and on some airlines, business class. Many corporations do not pay for business or first class because it is usually more expensive than coach. Business class and first class are roomier and more comfortable for longer flights, but more importantly, you may have an opportunity to network in business class. Use your frequent flier miles for upgrades or purchase upgrades if you wish to travel with more leg room and opportunity.

Practice proper etiquette and show courtesy to your seatmate(s), fellow passengers, and flight crew. Introduce yourself when you begin a conversation. Make sure your seatmate wants to chat before engaging her in conversation. She may need to prepare for a meeting or may prefer to relax quietly. When you do not wish to chat, politely tell your seatmate you have some business to prepare before you reach your destination (or that you'd like to read or relax), and excuse yourself from further talk.

Allow your seatmate(s) some elbow space on the armrest. Move your seat back slowly when you are ready to recline. Before using the air telephone, ask your seatmates if it will bother them. Speak softly when using the phone in flight. As you move about the airplane, use the magic words: please, thank you, and excuse me (see Chapter 6). Send a thank you note to the executive or other individual responsible for your travel arrangements when you return.

Corporate jets are used to transport corporate directors, clients, and management to important or urgent meetings. Corporate aircraft crew consists of a pilot, co-pilot, and occasionally a flight attendant. When traveling by corporate jet, arrive early so you do not delay departure. Wait to board until the hostess has arrived and boarded. Carry your own baggage unless the crew offers to store it for you. Space is usually limited so travel light (avoid using the plane to transport bulky purchases or personal items). Refreshments may be limited so accept what is offered without making requests that might embarrass the hostess or cause difficulty for the crew. Be neat so you aren't the sole cause for vacuuming the entire plane. When leaving the plane, thank the pilot and crew for the flight. Write a letter to the hostess and mention the crew. It is especially important to send a thank you note to the individual responsible for your corporate jet travel arrangements when you return.

If you are a frequent guest on the corporate jet, you may travel with the same crew. A card and gift are appropriate at holiday time and can be sent to the crew in care of the host.

Staying at a Hotel

Make reservations for your stay in a hotel in advance of your departure. Ask for any special accommodations you may need at the time you make your reservation. When you check in at the hotel, you may request a morning newspaper be delivered to your door, a wake up call, or a fresh pot of coffee or hot water for tea be delivered first thing in the morning.

Avoid conducting business meetings in your hotel room. It's no more appropriate to conduct a business meeting in your hotel room than it is in your bedroom at home. If your hotel suite has a separate living or meeting room, same gender meetings or meetings of four or more of mixed gender are acceptable.

Most hotels have lobbies suitable for meetings and even lobby lounges that are open most of the day. There are normally small tables provided for business papers. Leave the computer in its case; print reports before you meet. Hotel bars are generally noisy, dark, and unsuitable for quiet conversation for business. In some instances a quiet place may be found at a table on a restaurant patio between meal hours. I have seen informal meetings at a poolside table when there were few sunbathers or swimmers. Meetings with foreign guests should only be held in lobby lounges or hotel restaurants.

Most fine hotels provide toiletries as a convenience and a touch of luxury for their guests. Hotel robes, towels, and other items are not meant as gifts to be removed from the premises. Never take anything from your hotel room other than the toiletry samples. Other hotel items may be available from the gift shop for you to purchase. A monogrammed polo shirt from an upscale hotel might make a nice gift for a client who has enjoyed their stay in the hotel; purchase a new polo shirt from the gift shop and present it to your client on their departure.

For a complete discussion of gratuities see Chapter 3. A condensed version of the *Gratuity Guide* follows.

Mixed gender colleagues should not share a hotel room under any circumstances. Even in the most professional of relationships, the sharing of a room is likely to be interpreted negatively by clients and other business associates as well.

Use the in-room checkout where available. At check-in you will be asked to secure additional hotel charges with a credit card. Some hotels

Hotel maid	$1.00–1.50/day per person
Bellman or airport skycap	$1.00/bag
Concierge (for reservations, favors)	$2.00–20.00
Room service (service charged to bill)	$1.00–5.00 (in addition to service charge on the bill)
Parking valet (when you are leaving)	$1.00–3.00
Doorman (when he hails a cab for you)	$1.00–2.00
Taxi cab driver	10% of the bill

offer an expedited or express form of checkout that enables you to check out of the hotel without stopping at the front desk when you depart. Some hotels have a special TV channel for this purpose, others use different methods. Inquire about express checkout before your departure date. Often, hotels will allow you to settle your charges the evening before departure. Evening or in-room checkout is especially convenient if you have a very early departure time. Leave the room keys in a visible place in the room. Check the bill for accuracy before you check out. It will be easier for you to resolve any discrepancies now, before you leave the hotel, than it might be several days from now when you are back at your office and your memory is not so fresh.

Late checkout is sometimes available. If you have late meetings or a late flight you can request a late checkout eight to twenty-four hours before your departure. If the hotel can accommodate you, you can usually get an extension of an hour or two. Many hotels will be willing to grant your request. Housekeeping may be delayed in completing their block of room duties; provide an extra gratuity for their service (see the *Gratuity Guide*, Chapter 3).

When you are a frequent guest at a hotel chain, you may be offered special privileges of late checkout, room upgrades, free newspaper, and extra nights at no charge. You can benefit from planning your stays in one hotel chain and joining their member club.

Staying in a Private Home

Being invited to be a guest in a private home is an honor and requires special etiquette. Remember that you are a guest in someone's home; you are not in a hotel. Your host and hostess may have other responsibilities besides providing you with twenty-four-hour attention. Be considerate of their other commitments, time schedules, and privacy.

Select and bring an appropriate gift for your hosts. Your thoughtfulness will help set the tone for your stay. Gift baskets, edibles such as chocolates, and plants make fine gifts.

If you are asked to join your hosts for meals, be prompt and dress appropriately. You may need to inquire as to proper dress; some households are quite casual, others more formal. Naturally, use your best table manners.

Keep your room tidy; keep your clothes off the floor and make your bed when you arise. Hang your clothes in the closet or wardrobe and hang your towels.

Always use your telephone calling card for any phone calls you make using your host's phone. Be sure to ask before you use the phone.

Send a thank you note and flowers or plant within forty-eight hours of departure. Unless your host gives other instructions, leave a gratuity in an envelope for household help before you go.

Travel Safety

There are basic travel tips that can ensure safer travel and make your life easier. If at all possible, travel the day before the scheduled meeting. You will be at your best and be most effective after a good night's sleep, particularly if you travel some distance. Traveling the day before will also help to get your body attuned to the local time schedule.

Plan your travel schedule so you arrive in the new city before dark. You'll have an opportunity to see where you are going and to note nearby restaurants or other businesses you may need during your stay. Arriving during daylight hours may help you to secure a better hotel room while there are more choices. Later in the day, the hotel may not be as able to accommodate preferences such as a nonsmoking room or a room away from the traffic side of the building.

Prior to travel, inquire about the most efficient transportation to the hotel. Depending upon the time you arrive and your familiarity with the city, you may choose to use the hotel courtesy shuttle (if one is available), a cab or limousine service, or public transportation. Perhaps your client or their representative will plan to meet you at the airport or send a car for you.

Carry your contact's name and phone number in your wallet, just in case you are separated from your luggage. Luggage is sometimes misdirected to the wrong airport or put on a different flight and may take some time to catch up to you.

Select a hotel in a safe location. Ask your host or travel agent to recommend hotels in safe areas or close to your business destination (e.g., corporate office). A map of the local area might also be useful.

Cash, traveler's checks, and credit cards (and passport if you're traveling abroad) are safest carried in a secured money pouch. There are a variety of money belts or pouches; select one that suits you best. Some pouches are worn in the sock, the hem of a slip (undergarment), around the neck, on the shoulder, around the waist, or in a belt. The neck pouch is useful because it is easily accessible when you need important documents such as your passport and is easily hidden under a shirt or blouse.

One can never be too careful with money or valuables. Use the hotel safe for valuables, extra cash, and your passport. Be sure to ask about accessibility to the hotel safe so that you know when you can retrieve your property. Some hotels allow access to the safe only during specific hours. If your flight home is at 6 A.M. and the hotel safe doesn't open until 8 A.M., you'll need to ask for your valuables the evening before. Valuables that you must keep in your room, such as your computer or cell phone, are safest stored out of sight when not in use.

For your safety, hang the "Do Not Disturb" sign on your door at all times, and use the security lock on your door. Keep any windows secured; do not leave windows open at night or when away. Never let anyone into your hotel room whom you do not know or expect. This extends to hotel staff such as cleaning persons or room service. Be certain that the room phone in your hotel is in working order.

It is good practice to carry a flashlight with fresh batteries in your luggage. If there is a power failure in your hotel or an emergency such as a fire or natural disaster, you may need the flashlight to find your way out of your hotel. The guest speaker at a seminar in a hotel meeting room told a story about power failures that had been occurring in the part of the hotel where she was staying. She could still conduct the seminar meetings without electricity, but she needed her flashlight to go up and down the dark stairwell to her room between meetings. You should also make yourself familiar with the location of stairwells and emergency exit routes. Small night lights are also useful in hotel rooms.

When on an extended trip, especially one that takes you to multiple cities, plan to send papers back in a preaddressed, prestamped box or envelope. Your hotel may be able to assist you with shipping the materials back to your office. At most conference exhibits there are lots of materials for you to collect for later review. Plan to ship this material home rather than carry it through your travels. Literature and other materials collected at trade shows can get quite heavy. Shipping it home rather than carrying it will reduce your travel fatigue and perhaps free your hands for other items you need to carry while traveling.

Trade shows sometimes offer a carrying box that you can collect materials in and ship home after the show. Some trade shows also issue machine-readable plastic identification cards, similar to charge cards, each of which is encoded with the attendee's name and address. As you visit booths at the trade show, the exhibitors will run your card through an electronic machine that will later provide a mailing list so they can forward literature or other information you may have requested. This little card saves you from having to carry literature and saves the exhibitor from having to ship material and handle it at the show.

If you have attended a meeting where you have made a presentation and/or provided materials for your colleagues or clients, you may wish to discard unused presentation materials after your meeting rather than carry them back.

INTERNATIONAL TRAVEL

If you can gather information about the host's business and family prior to departure, you can plan to take gifts for the children such as team sport shirts and caps. Learn the geography and some pertinent facts about the country. You may want to obtain a map of the country to refer to during your travel. Take appropriate gifts (for a few ideas see the section on *Cultural Courtesy* in Chapter 8).

Learn a few words in the language. The magic words *please, thank you, hello,* and *good-bye* make a good start. Knowing how to count in the language is also helpful, especially as you begin to use the currency of the country.

Familiarize yourself with the monetary system. Your Sunday newspaper (travel or finance sections) may list the current exchange rates for the country you plan to visit. Plan to take at least $60 in foreign currency to cover immediate needs such as taxi cabs, bus rides, and tips. Frequently, the best exchange rates will be at the airport bank.

Plan to take appropriate clothing in neutral colors and conservative styles.

When you are a guest in another country act as a guest. Use your best manners.

Be on time. South of the U.S. border it is polite to be late to a business meeting by twenty minutes to an hour. More and more businesses, however, are encouraging their employees to be on time for meetings.

Plan to entertain your host in a restaurant. Ask your host or someone from your hotel to recommend an appropriate restaurant. Let your hosts know in advance that you wish to take them to dinner during your visit.

Be cautious about costs for entertaining. Plan your entertainment activities in advance so you are aware of the expense. Keep track of your time and expenses so you don't exceed your budget.

Chapter 10

After Hours

BUSINESS ENTERTAINING

Marketing, customer service, and employee appreciation are the most common reasons businesses entertain. A new product is being released and the company wants to make a big announcement about it. They invite all their clients and the press to an open house showcasing their newest product, complete with hors d'oeuvre and wine tasting. They distribute flashy literature and corporate memo pads and pens. All the employees are wearing custom polo shirts with fancy embroidered logos depicting the new product. Perhaps you've been to such an event. Most businesses either have a budget specifically for entertainment or at least an expectation that they will incur some entertainment expense, perhaps as a function of marketing or customer service.

Business entertainment may take a variety of forms. The most common form of entertainment is probably the business lunch or dinner. Some companies host parties, meetings, and seminars for staff and clients, while others host business meetings at restaurants. Some entertain their clients at sports events and community events. When you are entertained at one of these functions, be aware that you represent your business. Always show your professional polish and practice your power etiquette. Eating hot dogs and cheering at a baseball game does not free you of your professional responsibilities. In fact, you may be under assessment for a possible position in the company and are being entertained with the purpose of getting to know the "real you" more thoroughly!

The Invitation

Most corporate events begin with an invitation to attend. The invitation itself will usually yield a fair amount of information you need to know about the event: what it is for, the date it will be held and where, what kind of attire is required, and whether you are requested to let the host know that you plan to attend. The invitation may offer additional information as well, depending upon how formal or informal the invitation may be.

It is proper etiquette for you to respond to an invitation as soon as possible, certainly before the requested response date. Many invitations will ask for a response by marking the invitation, R.S.V.P., *répondez s'il vous plaît,* please respond. A thoughtful guest will respond even if the invitation is not so marked. Don't wait to be prompted by a response card or reminder. Practice your Power Etiquette. You have the responsibility to accept or decline when an invitation is extended to you. Make your decision within five days. You may write, call, e-mail, or respond in person. Check your calendar and if the date is open, accept, and mark your calendar to attend. Of course, emergencies do come up, but once you have made the commitment to attend, you should put that ahead of any later, perhaps more exciting invitation, for the same day. Your timely response to the invitation is more than just a formality. The host is trying to accurately determine how many guests will be attending in order to plan the food and activities, if any.

The bottom right of the invitation may indicate the suggested attire. Complying with it is not mandatory, but respectful to and considerate of the host. You are not likely to be refused entry, but you may be somewhat ostracized for your lack of compliance and sophistication. Your name may come up at the next board meeting in this negative context, or you might even be passed over for a promotion based on your inappropriate attire at the social function. You could be viewed as unsophisticated or ignorant of social propriety.

Prior to Attending

Did the invitation include you *and* a guest? If it is an evening or holiday event, when you accept you may ask if your invitation includes your spouse or significant other. The hostess may not be aware that you have recently married, have been married for some time, or have a significant other. Gently ask the host if you may bring your spouse or significant other. This is not the place to consider bringing a date or other guest if your hostess has not specifically indicated "and guest" in the original invitation.

If the invitation did not indicate any particular attire, or you are unsure for any reason, ask the hostess about the suggested attire. She would gladly advise you rather than allow you or her other guests to be embarrassed when you arrive improperly dressed. Plan your apparel for the occasion. It is generally better to be a bit overdressed than under-dressed. This is a business function, as well as a social one.

A hostess gift is almost always welcome and appreciated. The expense of your gift depends upon your relationship with the hostess. A hostess gift is really a thank you for the invitation and is intended to be enjoyed by the hostess after the party and the guests have departed. Be attentive to the implications your gift might convey in this business setting. Select something that is consumable, attractive, and not too personal. Soaps for the guest bath, holiday or theme guest towels, candles, food, coffee and tea, or gift baskets are always appreciated and appropriate. Be sure to include a social business card with a handwritten thank you for being invited to the event.

Entertainment Events

Types of business entertaining may include the following:

- ❖ A guest pass to your health club
- ❖ A golf match
- ❖ An evening at the theater or opera
- ❖ Attendance at a sports event
- ❖ An informal or formal tour of the city
- ❖ Sightseeing in the area
- ❖ An evening out on the town

- ❖ An open house with cocktails at your home
- ❖ A reception at a restaurant
- ❖ A pair of tickets to a local concert

Any of these might be appropriate for different business contacts, the advantage being their "softer" sell of the business side of the relationship. You are building a better working relationship, saying thank you, repaying a favor. Business talk may occur but the conversation is more relaxed and more likely to be fact finding.

When you entertain for business purposes, know the etiquette surrounding the form of entertainment you offer. Inviting your guest to a soccer game when you know nothing about soccer is foolish. Special sports events are commonly used for business entertaining. These are often used as a reward or thank you. Show your own etiquette skills and also your consideration of your guest by selecting an activity or event in which you are both interested.

For instance, golf has an etiquette and language all its own. Contact the golf course in advance if you have questions regarding acceptable attire. You will be expected to dress appropriately. You reserve a tee time, pay your green fees in advance, and begin your round of golf promptly. Swearing is poor etiquette at any time, as is throwing your golf club. You are to avoid talking when the others are preparing to swing. Naturally, this short paragraph could not possibly list all the nuances of etiquette of the age-old game of golf. However, if you and your business guest play golf, consider your handicap and avoid playing with someone who may have a much higher or lower one than yours. It could tax their patience and impair the goodwill of your meeting.

As you plan entertainment events for you and your guest, consider the other person's schedule and whether they have travel arrangements and accommodations to make. It is a gesture of courtesy to arrange lodging for any out-of-town guests. Let your guests know the appropriate attire for any event before the event. Your guests may need time to purchase and pack any needed clothing items.

After any event you attend for business, send a thank you note. A simple handwritten note or humorously worded e-mail message will do. You are acknowledging the host and the good time you shared at their event. Your host put time and energy into preparing an event and will appreciate your acknowledgment and thanks for their efforts.

Company Parties

As a guest at your company party, you are representing your company. Everything you say and do reflect on your company and your fellow employees.

- ❖ Avoid loud and/or inappropriate conversation.
- ❖ Wear conservative and appropriate clothing.
- ❖ Limit your alcohol consumption. Choose nonalcoholic beverages instead.
- ❖ Eat lightly and properly, observing the rules of proper etiquette for dining.
- ❖ Observe well and listen attentively.

Your good reputation precedes your arrival and is crucial to your career success. Always be alert to the impression you are leaving wherever you are and whatever you do. Is it a positive one?

> *At a company party I drank too much and flirted with the boss. Should I apologize in person or write a note of apology?*
> Avoid drawing attention to your errant behavior. If you openly embarrassed your employer, send an apology for having caused embarrassment.

Planning a Corporate Event

When you are selected to plan a company meeting, social event, new product celebration, or annual party you have a responsibility to put together the best event you possibly can. It will take your time and energy to succeed. You will devote extra work time to get the details in order. Whenever possible, ask for and get assistance.

The power of knowing what to do and being able to do it with ease creates an ambience in which both you and your corporate guests can be relaxed. When all participants can enjoy the event, you have succeeded in fostering good relations and giving positive experiences. These out of the office events are important in developing an appreciation of your varied skills, and the company, not only as a business but also as real people who care not just about the business, but about one another as well.

When you are put in charge of planning the next corporate or company event be aware of some basic considerations to. These begin with the reason for the event and the budget. These parameters must be clearly defined from the outset to make your planning successful.

The Caterer and Food

Finding a good caterer who understands your business needs and will work within your budget is a challenge. Find a quality caterer and you have a valuable asset and ally. The best way to find a caterer is by referral; ask friends or others who may have used a caterer recently. Also ask your colleagues and those in clubs and associations for referrals.

Interview the caterer to determine if he has the necessary skills and resources to serve your event; make sure it is someone with whom you can work well. As you begin planning the menu, ask for a sample tasting of possible selections.

Be clear about what you want and expect from your caterer. It is most professional and responsible to contract with the caterer and define all the details. Obtain a signed contract defining the date, location, and responsibilities and all charges, taxes, and tips (basic fees, corking fees, and any additional items). The contract should also list the caterer's licenses for preparing and serving food and alcohol. You may want to ask the caterer some of the following questions as well.

- ❖ Will the food be fresh or frozen?
- ❖ Is the food prepared fresh on-site or in advance at another location?
- ❖ Are they licensed for food preparation?

- ❖ Do they have an alcohol license?
- ❖ Do they observe responsible hospitality rules for safe serving?
- ❖ Do they carry liability insurance for themselves and their employees?
- ❖ Will there be adequate servers for the number of guests you expect and the type of event you have planned?
- ❖ What other accessories are available through the caterer, such as linens, tables, and glassware?
- ❖ Who is responsible for cleanup?
- ❖ When do we finalize the menu?
- ❖ When is the final head count due?

The cost of a catered event is normally based upon the number of people who will attend or a head count. The most accurate count will come from using an R.S.V.P. on your invitation. The final head count usually is taken a number of days before the event, as specified by your caterer, and you are responsible for payment for that number whether that number attends or not. Often the caterer will make some allowance for those who failed to R.S.V.P. and will add extra food; you may also have extra food when people who had planned to come do not attend. Be sure to send your invitations well in advance and ask for an R.S.V.P. or for Regrets Only (R.O.). Regrets Only is a request that your guests notify you only if they are unable to attend, otherwise they will be expected to attend.

You may select a location with your caterer, your caterer may suggest a location, or you may select one on your own. Visit the location in advance to confirm its suitability for the event. Make arrangements for the caterer to verify that she will be able to serve the food as required at the location selected. A sit-down dinner would be difficult to serve in a location that did not have access to a kitchen.

Your caterer may also be able to help with decorations. If not, you'll need to make other arrangements for your event decorations. Make arrangements both for seating and standing; again, your caterer may be able to help. Either way, there are a number of details of this nature that you will need to think of and plan for to have a successful event.

Corporate Event or Meeting Planners

You can be the event planner yourself and handle all the details, or you may choose to work with a professional event or meeting planner. You can leave as much or as little planning to the planner as you wish. As you might expect, the higher the level of involvement, the higher the fee. Fees for event arranging for a group of one hundred people can run from $800 to $5,000 (not including the costs of catering the event), depending upon your area and the type of event you want.

The event planner should be chosen based on their previous record of planning similar events. Ask for referrals and call them to discuss their experience with the event planner. Your choice should be by recommendation or personal experience. Whether you plan the event yourself, or use an event planner, allow six weeks or more for the planning.

GIFTING

Corporate or business gifting should be carefully planned and prepared ahead of the time for gifting. Holidays are the normal time for giving gifts. You may wish to gift during the year for other reasons, such as a thank you for a contract or client referral. Gifting is a common corporate and business practice. There should be guidelines for the person who makes the gift decisions and purchases. Establish a policy for gifting, put it in writing, and follow it. Consistency is important to gifting.

When gifting policies are written, the procedures can be maintained by succeeding individuals who take over the responsibility. Sometimes corporations purchase logo gifts for holidays and specific gifts for other occasions. At other times gifts are individually purchased. The ease of gifting can be achieved with planning and preparation to make gifting fun rather than a burden. Care must be taken to observe the proper rules of etiquette in gift giving.

Special gift cards or enclosures may be preprinted and should always be included with any gift. Company sentiments and signatures should be uniform for all gifts. Thought should be given as to how the cards are signed, whether by the whole staff, the CEO and staff, individual names, or the corporate name alone.

Whatever gift you chose to give, make no attempt to commercialize your product or service. Be sensitive about giving sample products and certificates for your products. Likewise be vigilant that you do not inadvertently promote a competitor's business.

A business logo included on the gift creates a lasting reminder of your business relationship. Each situation for gifting must be evaluated for the appropriateness of a logo gift. A wedding gift to a client or employee with a logo is not appropriate, whereas a holiday gift with a logo is appropriate.

Not all gift items are well suited to logos. You must consider the shape and color of your logo to achieve the most successful effect. Specialty suppliers may be able to recommend items best suited to your logo shape, clients, and budget. Listed below are good items for most logos:

- Clothing
- Clocks
- Phone cards
- Desk accessories
- Beverage mugs
- Luggage tags
- Self-stick notes or notepads
- Pens and pencils
- Golf tees and divot repair tools
- Hand calculators
- Date books or calendars
- Etched beverage glasses
- Ice buckets
- Magnets
- Key rings
- Letter openers

Any of these items may have your logo and company information on them. Your gift selection should be made based on something you would be pleased to receive or that might be in line with your products or services. I know of a shipping company that gave box openers as gifts. To express your professionalism choose practical, nonoffending, personalized gifts that express your thoughtfulness and consideration and appreciation of your business association.

Timing is always a consideration. Timeliness is evidence of your attention to detail and consideration. Send holiday gifts one to two weeks before the holiday. A one- to two-week window before and after other events, such as for wedding or congratulatory gifts, is also appropriate.

Be cognizant of the cultural background or dietary preferences of the intended recipient and select your gift accordingly. You may always refer to international gifting guides for suggestions or call the embassy or consulate near you.

Your gift is most effective when sent as close to the event it celebrates as possible. Sending a gift a month after the anniversary date is too late, but a month after the fact is not too late to celebrate a promotion. You'll need to use good judgment and send the gift as early as possible. Gifts are appropriate for many occasions and events.

- ❖ Congratulations
- ❖ Graduation
- ❖ Promotion
- ❖ Significant birthday year
- ❖ Receiving an award (if it benefits your copany)
- ❖ New job or opening a new office
- ❖ Work-related anniversary
- ❖ Changing careers
- ❖ Job of a service provider
- ❖ Hosting you in another city
- ❖ Apologies
- ❖ For unintentionally offending someone
- ❖ Birth of a baby
- ❖ Wedding
- ❖ Retirement
- ❖ Thank you
- ❖ For extraordinary work
- ❖ Appearance on TV (if it generates business for you)
- ❖ Notable achievement
- ❖ Relocating to another city
- ❖ Buying a new home
- ❖ Doing a favor
- ❖ Hosting you at a special event
- ❖ For a misunderstanding
- ❖ Forgetting/failing to attend an important event

If an office colleague or business client invites you to a wedding, christening, graduation, bat or bar mitzvah, a gift is generally in order. Even if you cannot attend, you should send a gift and acknowledge the event. If you have not received a thank you within ninety days, you may inquire as to whether the gift was received. If you are the gift recipient, proper etiquette requires you to send your thank you notes promptly.

Don't go empty-handed to a dinner party, open house, cocktail party, or holiday party. The value of the gift is not as important as the thought. A plant, a loaf of homemade bread, or a simple gift pack of tea or coffee is appropriate. The host should not be encouraged to open the gift upon receipt. If you wish to share in their joy when they receive the gift, wrap the gift in clear cellophane and tie it with a pretty bow. Always attach a card and handwritten message so the hostess can respond to the appropriate person.

Keep in mind that not everyone can accept gifts. Take care that the gift is appropriate for the business relationship. Lavish gifting can create awkwardness. Gifts given for business purposes may be tax deductible; check with your accountant or the appropriate tax code for details. Be sure to keep detailed records of gifts and recipients for your business records.

Creative gifts are always well received. Consider a gift basket of consumable products such as dried fruit and nuts, chocolates, or specialty coffees or teas. A magazine subscription for an area the recipient is interested in would be welcomed. A woman I know repaired and restored a special display box for a client, simply as a favor since it was her hobby. The client ordered a subscription to a hobby magazine as a thank you for the work. You might also consider making a contribution to a favorite charity in the person's name or perhaps to a local soup kitchen or self-help center. Gift certificates from local department stores or restaurants also make thoughtful gifts.

You may give special colleagues a homemade gift of vinegar, jam, tea, bread, cookies, or a handmade holiday ornament. A card with a personal note expressing your appreciation for their business association and sending your good wishes is *always* appropriate and appreciated.

The Gift List

Deciding who should be on your gift list shouldn't be too big of a challenge. Look through your date book or keep a running list of people you worked with during the year. Review the year's events. Make a list of all those who helped make your year a success. Don't overlook the supplier who met your early deadline and the colleagues who gave extra effort on a joint project.

Should I give my boss a holiday gift?
Do not gift above your company rank. Your intentions for gifting may be misunderstood. A gift may be given to the boss if it is from the entire staff.

Gift Presentation

Several gift catalogues and stores offer a consultant to assist with the selection, purchase, wrapping, and delivery of corporate gifts. Every gift should be wrapped nicely. How the gift is presented may have more meaning to the receiver than the gift itself. Use a favorite color or print for the wrapping paper and other package decoration.

How and when the gift is presented should be a major consideration. Giving a useful travel gift a week prior to departure is sensible, but not after the bags are packed. A gift of fruit and a card placed in the hotel room before arrival is nicer than a bottle of champagne the day before departure.

A holiday gift was sent to my office. Is it appropriate to
e-mail the thank you?
If someone has taken the time to send a gift to you, proper etiquette dictates that you should take the time to respond with a handwritten note. Everyone is busy, especially during the holidays. Of course, an immediate e-mail acknowledgment and thank you is acceptable when followed by your handwritten note.

Gift Ideas

For CEOs, VIPs, and Senior Executives (value: over $200)

Case of wine
(a frequent gift from one
CEO to another CEO)

Sports equipment
(golf, ski, scuba diving)

Antique desk or office
accessories

Personal use items
(electronic gadgets)

Designer accessories
(scarf, gloves, briefcase)

Fountain pen

Sports tickets

(continued)

(*continued*)

Theater tickets	Crystal glassware
Art work	Books of special interest
(painting, sculpture)	to the recipient

For Middle Managers, Junior Executives, and Business Peers (value: $50–$100)

Gift certificates	Music tapes/CDs
Desk items	Gourmet food items
Gourmet cheeses	Gourmet chocolates
Memberships to museums	Books
Sports equipment accessories	Electronic accessories

For Office Personnel, Support Staff (value $20–$50)

Gift certificates	Desk accessories
Books of personal or	Magazine subscription for
business interest	special interest
Quality pen/pencil sets	Music tapes/CDs
Ticket to favorite event	Crystal pieces
Clocks	Gourmet food baskets
Photo frames	Electronic gadgets
Fruit or pastry of the month	
selection	

Inappropriate Gift Items for Any Business Purpose

Expensive jewelry	Religious items
Sports equipment to	Wine or liquor to
nonathletes	nondrinkers
Perfume or perfumed items	Animals
Intimate apparel	Items with sexual overtones
Any item of inferior quality	

ACCEPTING GIFTS

The graceful acceptance of a gift is a gift in itself. Whenever you accept a gift from a colleague or business associate you enable them to experience the pleasure that comes from giving. You also acknowledge and accept their thoughtfulness and goodwill towards your business relationship. A thank you note is always appropriate to thank a giver for a business-related gift.

Can I refuse a gift or return it?

You may return a gift when it violates your company policy to accept a gift or when the gift is above your company gift acceptance value limit. You may also return a gift if the gift is inappropriate for your business relationship with the giver, is too personal (as jewelry or undergarments), or is of excessive value. A gift from a giver known to expect favors in return or who makes you feel obligated in any way may be returned. You should also return a gift if you have a pending business contract with the giver.

To refuse the gift, it must be returned within twenty-four hours and sent with a handwritten note stating that the company forbids your accepting gifts or that it is inappropriate for you to accept. Return the gift by a delivery company that requires a signature of acceptance. You do not need to telephone the giver before returning it, nor should the subject be part of any future conversations. If the giver mentions the incident, state again the reason you gave for returning the gift in the note and drop the subject.

COMMUNITY INFLUENCE

Your position of responsibility and your ability to influence both people and decisions affects others both within and beyond the workplace. Your self-esteem and feelings of self-worth can be greatly enhanced when you can give the gifts of your time and experience to benefit others. Your skills can make a difference in the community where you work and live.

Participate in associations connected to your trade and business. Cultivate opportunities to serve on local community projects or with nonprofit and volunteer groups. You'll become known as a contributor to the betterment of the community and as a reliable and responsible individual. Your sphere of influence will grow to the benefit of both your personal and professional lives. The most content and successful business people are the ones who give back to their communities. Studies show that of the highly successful and satisfied business leaders, over 80 percent are involved in nonprofit community service.

A proven and effective business leader will be asked to use those same skills in volunteer positions. You are likely to be asked to serve on boards and committees. Wherever you are, use all your courteous and respectful manners. Power Etiquette involves the consistent and continual practice of proper etiquette; good etiquette skills are not employed in one occasion and dismissed in another.

Volunteer Service

Are you ready to serve your community? The volunteer center or community foundation can provide you with suggestions as to where you are needed or where your skills might best be put to work. There are many organizations, eager for new volunteers, that could benefit from your skills. Select one that has meaning and interest to you. Going out and volunteering just anywhere will provide little value to you personally, to your career, or to the community.

Volunteering can help your career. Company values vary, and volunteer work can often help your career or a possible promotion. You will develop new skills and develop relationships with others that may bring new opportunities your way. Choose organizations that are recognized as solid, goal-orientated concerns that offer volunteer hours for after-work activity. Never use company time for your volunteer commitments unless your company sponsors volunteering during company time. You will have a personal sense of fulfillment when you are giving back to the community.

There is no excuse for bad manners or stepping on others. We all need to be acknowledged, respected, and needed, and generally in that order. In all your business relationships, whether in the course or your work or your volunteer service, consider ways in which you can acknowledge, respect, and help others feel as though they are contributors to the positive welfare of others.

Leadership Service

One way to serve the community is to serve on a board of directors. Every nonprofit organization needs competent people to serve and volunteer their time to help steer the future of the organization. You can use your special expertise in the role of a board member. Many business people serve as members of boards of directors, lending their experience and ideas to the goals of the organization. There you can use your specific skills for fund-raising, crunching numbers, public relations, and so forth. You will always work more effectively and derive more personal satisfaction when you give your time and talent to serve a project about which you feel deeply.

If you have leadership skills you may be asked to serve as an officer such as vice president or president. Be sure that you understand the commitment of time and responsibility before you undertake the task. Some terms of office are for two or three years.

Whenever you serve as an officer, use the suggestions for conducting a project meeting following *Robert's Rules of Order* (see *Chairing a Meeting*, Chapter 7).

As you encourage others, be sensitive to the fears that many will have about taking on leadership responsibility and speaking in front of others. To demonstrate your confidence in them, show and explain as many details about the position as you can. It is helpful to have ready information about future meeting dates, specific responsibilities, time commitments, and suggestions for improvement. Be honest about the time and effort needed for the office or any project.

If you are an outgoing officer, prepare a folder of duties and information for the incoming officer who will be taking on your responsibilities. A simple outline of responsibilities makes the job transition smoother. The new officer will appreciate your effort and courtesy. The slate of officers will be easier to fill when you can courteously provide candidates with as much information as possible.

As the program chair responsible for arranging outside programs, plan as far ahead as you can to fill the programs. There are several resources for guest speakers: Toastmasters International and the National Speakers Association both have members who are eager to speak to your group. You can also ask for suggestions from members. Contact the speakers you are interested in, get the speaker's address, as well as her fax and e-mail address, send a confirmation letter for your event, send past and current newsletters, and confirm with the speaker prior to the meeting. Provide each speaker with the details of location, arrival time, length of program, number of expected guests, and age range of the attendees. Fax or send them a map. Pay any honorarium or make a donation to the speaker's preferred local charity in a timely manner and provide a small thank you gift.

You may be asked to serve on the nominating committee for an organization. You may be in charge of recruiting new officers to a board or for an organization. If you are on the nominating committee to select new officers, endeavor to select new officers with the same sensitivity with which you would hire a new employee. As you recruit new officers, be sensitive to the fears that many people have about taking on responsibility and speaking in front of others. Remind yourself that you are serving the organization and not yourself. If you can encourage others to serve, show them the forms that are ready for use, explain as many details as you can about future meeting dates, their responsibilities, and the required time commitment. Also ask for suggestions for other individuals who might serve as officers. Always be honest about the time and effort needed to fulfill the responsibilities of the office.

Your Challenge:
To Be the Best You Can Be

*P*racticing proper business etiquette is powerful.

Now that you have finished reading this book, reflect on how you have conducted yourself in various business settings. In what situations has your business etiquette been completely proper? What business situations could you have handled more appropriately? What aspects of business conduct are confusing and need clarification? In what situations do you feel totally comfortable and in control? Do your clients and colleagues enjoy your company and you theirs?

Reflecting on the above questions and honestly assessing your conduct in all types of business functions will move you toward the goal of practicing Power Etiquette. Knowing what is proper conduct allows you to be comfortable and in control in any business situation. Your poise and confidence will reflect your leadership abilities, and both your reputation and that of your company's for superb client relationships will soar. Your manners are always on display. How you conduct yourself in your relationships with other people will determine your future success. The courtesies you extend to those around you will come back to you a hundredfold. Those courtesies will be remembered and savored by your contacts, and those contacts will ensure your future success. Accept the challenge of continually improving your business etiquette, and your life will be richer and more fulfilling because of the many friendships you will cultivate along life's path.

Manners open doors that position and money cannot.

Bibliography of
International Customs

Communicating with Customers Around the World
K.C. Chan-Herur, AuMonde International Publishing Co.,
San Francisco, 1994

Do's and Taboos Around the World, 3rd Edition
Roger Axtell, John Wiley & Sons, New York, 1993

Do's and Taboos Around the World for Women in Business
Roger Axtell, John Wiley & Sons, New York, 1997

Do's and Taboos of Hosting International Visitors
Roger Axtell, John Wiley & Sons, New York, 1991

Gestures
Roger Axtell, John Wiley & Sons, New York, 1991

Going International
Lennie Copeland and Lewis Griggs, A Plume Book by arrangement with
Random House, 1985

Kiss, Bow, or Shake Hands: How to Do Business in Sixty Countries
Terri Morrison, Wayne A. Conaway, and George A. Borden, Adams
Publishing, 1994

Passport to the World Series
Your Pocket Guide to Business, Culture and Etiquette. World Trade Press,
1997–98. Currently twenty-three books on specific countries in print.

A Simple Guide to (name of the country)
Customs and Etiquette in ___, Customs and Etiquette Series. Global Books
Ltd., England 1995. Distributed by The Talman Co., New York.

Index

About the Author

Dana May Casperson is a member of National Speakers Association. As a professional speaker she conducts her "Manners Matter" etiquette seminars internationally for professionals, sports teams, teens, and children. For the past ten years her personalized programs have assisted thousands of people – including underprivileged youth nationwide – gain the ability to be confident and comfortable anywhere in the world.

Casperson's extensive knowledge of fashion, tea, and cosmopolitan cultures makes her a delightful keynote speaker for luncheon or dinner occasions where she discusses the dos and don'ts of dining etiquette with polish and panache.

As a manners maven, Dana May prefers the civility of drinking afternoon tea to the three martini lunch. Her popular "Etiquette Teas" have proven to be effective fundraising events for people of all ages. She coauthored a booklet "The Story of Tea." Dana May welcomes your inquiries on "Manners Matter" programs or a tea brochure.

Contact her at: POB 3637
Santa Rosa, CA 95402-3637
(707) 579-4367 or
danamay@authoritea.com